Richard Potts was born in 1938 and left school at the age of sixteen. He spent four years as an apprentice draughtsman, and did his National Service as a nursing orderly in the RAF. He then took a degree in education at Keele University. *The Haunted Mine* is his second book, and has been serialized on the BBC Television programme, *Jackanory*. His first book is *An Owl for his Birthday*. He now teaches in York, and is married with three children.

THE HAUNTED MINE

RICHARD POTTS

Cover illustration by A. S. Knight
Text illustrations by Charles Keeping

A Piccolo Book

PAN BOOKS LTD
LONDON

First published 1968 by Lutterworth Press
This edition published 1973 by Pan Books Ltd,
33 Tothill Street, London SW1

ISBN 0 330 23750 0

For my mother and father
and John

Printed in Great Britain by
Richard Clay (The Chaucer Press), Ltd, Bungay, Suffolk

Contents

THE HAUNTED MINE

CHAPTER ONE

The Mine

IT STOOD alone against the sky, unused, like a protectionless, battered scarecrow, ageing as time passed. Mortar crumbled from between the bricks and scattered like bird droppings below. The tall chimney appeared to sway from side to side as fast-moving clouds scudded low, almost touching the black top.

For generations it had been the centre, the heartbeat, of a community. Now that community had been outfaced by new bungalows. The mine was all that remained, remembered as it had been only by the old men who sat on park benches. There was a sadness about the mine; like the old men, its years were numbered. One day it would crumble back into the earth from which it had come. But that day had not arrived, and if it was ignored and forgotten, there were two people to whom it meant more than a scar on the landscape.

They were two brothers, who would have been able to see the mine from their bedroom window, if another house had not blotted out the view. By standing on a chair they could just glimpse the topmost bricks of the chimney.

Their names were Max and Ben Davidson. Max was eleven. He was tall and thin, his face lit up by things he planned to do. His head was covered by a mop of blond curls, which sometimes made strangers mistake him for a girl. Ben, his younger brother by a year, was almost a foot shorter, and though he was not fat, when he stood next to Max everything about him was round. His face, his body, even his ears which jutted straight outwards appeared round.

It was a Sunday afternoon at the beginning of September. Ben was lying on the double bed which almost filled their small room. He was reading a comic, his hands cupped to his head, his legs in the air. Now and then he shifted his position, licked a finger to his lips, and turned the pages of the comic.

Max was standing by the window gazing out into the back garden. He was watching his mother, who was by the low wire fence which divided the bungalows. She was talking to the people next door. They were called Johns. Mr Johns was almost bald, his hair was white, and his face was brown even in winter-time. He didn't go to work; he never did anything except weed the garden and smoke his pipe. Max and Ben didn't like him.

He never spoke to them, and if one of their balls went into his garden they rarely had it returned. Max and Ben didn't like Mrs Johns either. Except when she was cooking the meals or cleaning the house, which was spotless, she liked nothing better than to tell stories about other people. She knew everybody's business. If Max and Ben ever did anything they shouldn't have done, she could always be relied upon to inform Mum.

She was telling a story now. She was leaning forward and whispering into Mum's ear. Max pulled a face and then looked down at his brother on the bed. He didn't like Ben reading when he himself had nothing to do. That afternoon the brothers were not friends. Max had been in trouble at lunch-time for not eating his dinner. Of course perfect little Ben had left his plate clean.

Max gazed round the room. There wasn't a great deal to see. Above the bed was a picture of Dad's ship. Dad was in the Navy and he had been at sea for nearly a year. On the chair by the window was Ben's tattered, brown Teddy-bear. Next to the chair was a scratched and ink-stained dressing-table, which was cluttered with dirty handkerchiefs and discarded sweet packets.

Suddenly, without warning, Max took a flying leap and landed on top of his brother. The comic tore in two. Ben fought like a tiger, but Max was the stronger. Soon Max was sitting on his chest. Ben's arms were pinned to his side. He kicked, but he wasn't able to reach far enough to put a lock on his brother's head.

When he realized he couldn't do it he went for Max's hand with his teeth. Max took hold of Ben's hair and pulled his head back.

'Ouch,' Ben protested.

'Do you submit?' Max yelled in his ear. Ben didn't answer. He struggled violently, swinging Max from side to side. But he wasn't able to throw him off. Sweat poured over him, sticking to his clothes. He let his body go, panting like a dog. Max took advantage of this. He moved forward on Ben's chest, squashing Ben's shoulder-blades flat on to the bed.

'Submit,' he hissed through his teeth. Ben lay limp, staring up into his brother's face.

'Submit,' Max ordered a second time.

'You're hurting my arm,' Ben moaned. 'Get off. Get off me.'

'Not till you submit,' Max told him. He began slapping Ben's cheeks, half seriously, half in fun.

'Submit. Submit. Submit. Submit,' he chanted. Ben swung his face in an attempt to avoid the blows.

'I'll tell Mum,' he wailed. Max went on slapping his face until Ben really did cry. Then he rolled on to the floor. He stared at Ben, not quite sure whether he had hurt him or not.

'Great bully,' Ben whimpered. He jumped to his feet and stumbled towards the door. Max realized what was happening too late. By the time he had started after him Ben was into the living-room. Ben had almost reached the kitchen when he slipped on the wet tiled floor. Before he could pick himself up, Max pulled his

shirt out, knocked him to the ground and sat on his head.

Mum must have heard the scuffle. She flung open the door and marched into the kitchen. She was a huge woman. She was almost six feet in height and she weighed seventeen stone. Max and Ben disentangled themselves. They tried to run round her legs but they hadn't a chance. The door was shut. Mum had her foot against it.

'Now you listen to me,' her voice boomed out, her finger wagging in front of their faces. 'If I catch you fighting in my kitchen once more I'll knock the stuffing out of the pair of you.'

'It wasn't me, Mum,' Ben complained, 'I was reading my comic and Max tore it up.'

'He wouldn't play with me,' Max retorted.

'I'm not interested who started it,' Mum shouted, her voice rising to its full pitch. 'The next time you dirty my kitchen floor I'll rub your noses in it. Do you understand?' Both boys meekly nodded their heads. Neither spoke. They knew the row would be over quicker if they said nothing.

'Then outside, this instant,' she said, raising her hand as if to hit them. Max and Ben scrambled to their feet and made for the door.

'And remember this,' she called after them. Ben obediently turned to face her.

'Those presents your father is sending. They'll be here any day. If there's any more hanky-panky I'll give them to an orphanage.'

Max and Ben looked at each other in horror.

'Oh. Please, Mum. No,' Max pleaded.

'Be off with you,' she said. As she spoke she moved towards them. Max tore open the door and they both escaped into the driveway.

Mr and Mrs Johns were standing by the fence.

'A good hiding is what those children need,' Mr Johns said thoughtfully, lighting his pipe. Mrs Johns nodded her head wisely in agreement.

'Hooligans,' she muttered, loud enough for Max and Ben to hear. Then she went inside, a duster under her arm.

Max and Ben hurried along the street, their shoes ringing out on the pavement. Most people were out of their houses, cleaning cars, laying concrete, erecting fences, weeding gardens or just talking to each other. The boys felt they were being watched, as if everybody knew they had been in trouble. The little girl who lived three doors away from them pedalled furiously past on her tricycle. She stuck out her tongue, turned round and went back to her friends.

It was a relief when they reached the edge of the estate. They crossed the waste ground where more new houses were being built. The mine loomed up in front of them, dominating the barren landscape. To one side there was the railway embankment. Every half hour the electric trains rattled past on their way to town. Between the houses and the mine there were a series of slackheaps. They were like miniature mountains. Dots of grass and weed sprouted out of them. Otherwise they were dead. It was not often that one saw birds in this area. Between the first two mountains there was a crater, which, except on dry summer days, was full of water.

Max ran on ahead, his heart lifting up. He picked up flat pieces of slate and skimmed them through the air. Ben chased after him. The ground rose up and down. It was rather like riding on a switch-back railway.

Soon they were standing on the top of the first mountain. The crater was below them. It was dull and black and it stood perfectly still. Unlike any other lake, nothing grew at the water's edge.

Max and Ben raced down the slope. They found long sticks and began prodding the black slime on the bed of the lake. Ben brought up a rusted, empty tin. He swung the tin round and dashed it down. Water splashed over them both. Max picked up a large stone and hurled it into the water near to where Ben was standing. They both howled with laughter. It was not long before they were soaked to the skin. They climbed back to the rim of the crater and sat next to each other, pleased with what they had achieved. A warmth of feeling passed between them.

'We can't go home like this,' Max said, examining his brother's clothing, 'not after the row we've just been in.' He slapped Ben on the back. Ben slapped him. Clouds of coal dust rose round them.

'You're like a coal man,' Ben giggled. Both thought of Mum at the same moment.

'It must be tea-time,' Ben said seriously. They

glanced towards the rows of bungalows which stood out against the smokey afternoon sky.

'It's not dark yet. It can't be that late.'

'We have to go home some time,' Ben said.

'Let's see the mine,' Max suggested nonchalantly.

'You promised Dad we never would,' Ben reminded him.

'I know we promised,' Max said crossly, 'but he'll not find out.'

'He'd be angry with us,' Ben argued.

'I tell you he'll never know,' Max said, impatient of his brother's babyness.

'I'm not going,' Ben told him sulkily. He wanted to go. Ever since they had moved to the new estate he had wanted to. But they had promised Dad before he sailed on his ship. Dad was in Australia now and it wasn't fair to break promises, not promises like that. 'Nobody's ever to know,' Max said, his voice softly persuasive. 'Go on. I'll let you sleep by the wall tonight if you come with me.'

Ben hesitated. Max put an arm round his shoulder, a thing he only did when he wanted to please his brother.

'Well, all right,' Ben agreed, 'but we mustn't go too close to the mine. We'll just throw stones at the tower.' When Max was kind and looked after him he would do anything for him.

'Come on, then,' Max said, his voice no longer so patient.

'And promise you won't tell Mum we have been.'

'I promise,' Max shouted angrily, 'now come on and stop being so frightened.'

'I don't like it when you shout at me,' Ben said peevishly.

'Now then, there, there, my little brother.' Max gave him a bear hug, lifted him off the ground and swung him around and around. He tickled Ben under the armpits. Ben struggled and they almost fell into the crater of the lake.

Max took Ben's hand and they danced along the slackheaps towards the mine. A train tore down the railway line. They threw themselves flat on the ground, afraid someone might recognize them from one of the train windows. The engine hooted and disappeared amongst the houses.

When they stood up the light seemed suddenly to have gone darker.

'Mum will be worrying about us,' Ben said, 'we ought to go home.' He was aware he was being a sissy but he couldn't help himself. Max took his hand again and pulled him on.

'We're nearly there. It would be stupid to go back now we've come this far.'

In fact they were almost there. When they reached the top of the next mountain the mine stood stark and silent in front of them. Ben clasped Max's hand. He wanted to go back, he desperately wanted to go back, but he knew if he complained Max would be angry with him. Their friendly moments were so rare. It caused him pain every time they quarrelled.

They stared up at the massive red brick building and at the chimney which towered from it into the sky. A few feet away from the building was a low, circular, brick structure, in the centre of which was the mine-shaft. Round it there had once been a fence, but the wire holding the palings had come loose and little remained of it now. To one side stood a battered notice-board, crooked and rotting. The paint had peeled from it years ago and all that was left of the printing were the five letters DANGE.

Max was frightened. Now they were here he felt isolated. Other people had ceased to exist. Yet he would not allow his fear to be conveyed to Ben. He steeled his arms to prevent them from shaking.

'Come on, Ben,' he said. 'Let's see who can hit the chimney first. Then we'll go home.' His voice rang out strangely in this wasteland. He picked up a lump of slate and skimmed it through the air, but it missed by a mile. Ben took up a stone, encouraged at being called by his Christian name. He threw with all his might. The stone went straight towards the chimney and for one moment Ben thought he had made a hit, but it fell short and rolled back down the slackheap.

'Bet I beat you,' Max boasted. He ran forward and threw again. Soon they were panting and perspiring. For a while Ben forgot his fear. Here was a chance for him to show Max he was his equal. But he didn't succeed, for with his next stone Max landed right in the middle of the chimney stack.

'Hard cheese,' Max said, pleased that he had won.

He dusted his trousers and then licked the palms of his hands clean with his tongue. 'Suppose we had better go,' he added. Ben was relieved. Darkness was almost on them. Something terrible would happen if they stayed at the mine. Ben was certain it would. As they ran back across the slackheaps he was positive he heard footsteps behind them, but he dared not stop to see if it was only an echo of themselves.

They came to the lake, and skirted round it, the cold black water below them.

'Let's walk the rest of the way,' Max said. 'We don't want Mum to think there's anything wrong.'

The street lights twinkled ahead. Through a kitchen window they could see a woman ironing.

Mum was waiting for them in the middle of the road. She stood by herself, a coat wrapped loosely about her shoulders. She did not move or speak till they reached her.

'Where have you been?' she asked, her voice tired and choking with tears.

'We've only been playing on the building-site,' Max lied innocently.

Ben nodded his head, ashamed they were deceiving her when she was upset. He took her hand and pulled her down to him.

'I'm sorry, Mum,' he whispered into her ear.

'It's all right, Ben,' she said. 'It doesn't matter now I know you are safe.' Max trudged behind, a scowl on his face. It was always Ben who managed to say the things which pleased her.

The street was quiet except for the distant clanging of church bells. Their front door was open. The light from the hall fell on the lawn. They slunk into the living-room, dust falling from their clothes on to the carpet. The television was switched on. Pages from the Sunday newspapers were scattered on the floor. Tea was laid on the table by the window. There was a half-eaten slice of bread on Mum's plate and steam rose from her cup.

Max and Ben turned to Mum as she came in through the door. They stood facing her, waiting for the row. But it did not come. She switched off the television with a quick jerk, went into the bathroom and ran the water.

'How did you ever get so much dirt on you?' was the only reproach she made.

'We had a race round the building-site and we fell over. That's all, Mum,' Max explained. She shrugged her shoulders, led them into the bathroom and helped them undress. She scrubbed their necks and washed their hair. Then she went to the kitchen to make their tea. Neither Max nor Ben spoke. They knew they had done wrong and there was nothing to say about it.

Ben felt warm and happy inside. Max and he were friends and Mum was being kind to them. He stayed in the bath after Max had climbed from the black, scum-covered water. He lay submerged to his chin, watching the globules of water on the walls and ceiling. The mine seemed far away. He was no longer afraid. He could hear Mum singing in the kitchen and that made him feel safe.

A short time later she called, 'Hurry up, Ben. The eggs are boiling.' Ben jumped out of the bath, shivering in the cold night air which blew in through the open window. He quickly dressed in his pyjamas, pulled out the plug and wiped the bath clean with the old sponge.

He remembered to fold the towels and lay them neatly over the rail on the door.

The curtains were drawn in the front room. It was warm and cosy. Mum had made a pot of fresh tea and she was pouring it into their cups. Ben sat next to Max at the table. He broke the top off his egg. It was soft and runny, just how he liked it. Mum sat in her armchair by the electric fire, picked up her knitting and watched them eat.

'You mustn't frighten me like that; not when Daddy isn't here,' she said suddenly.

'No,' Max answered sheepishly.

'I don't know what to do when I'm on my own,' she went on. Max avoided her gaze, but Ben looked her in the eyes and said, 'We won't let it happen again, Mummy, I promise we won't.'

Max stared at the patterns on the carpet. He hated Ben calling her 'Mummy', and it embarrassed him when she talked to them like this.

'Come and sit over here,' she said, 'and we'll forget all about it.' She put her arms round them and gave a friendly squeeze. Ben snuggled up close to her. Max accepted the hug, then stood up and went over to the television.

'Can we have the film on?' he asked.

'Not tonight, Max. Anyway it's nearly your bedtime.' Max pursed his lips, picked up the newspaper and thumbed through it.

'Your presents might come tomorrow,' Mum reminded them.

'What do you think they'll be, Mummy?' Ben asked excitedly.

'You wait and see, Ben,' she answered, patting his arm, 'but they will be coming all the way from Australia, so I want you to remember to write to Daddy's ship and thank him.'

'Oh. We will, Mummy, you know we will,' Ben told her. Max screwed up his face in disgust.

Later in bed he pushed Ben on to the floor as an act of revenge. Ben picked himself up and tore Max's pillow from under his head. 'You promised I could sleep by the wall tonight,' he cried to Max. '"You promised",' Max said, mimicking Ben's high-pitched voice. Ben brought the pillow crashing down on his brother's head. The blow sent Max sprawling to the other side of the bed. He lay still on his back, listening for Mum getting out of her chair. When there was no sound from the next room, he gave a broad grin, snatched the pillow from Ben's grasp and flailed him with it.

Max chuckled. He hadn't finished with his little brother yet. He tiptoed across the room, drew the curtains and then switched off the light. Ben knew what was coming. He couldn't bear the dark. He climbed back into the bed, pulled the sheets over his head and listened. There was the pad of Max's bare feet on the linoleum. Ben held his body tense. He wanted to shout for Mum, but if he did she might be angry and Max would be his enemy for the rest of the holidays.

Nothing happened. There was no sound, except for the voices from the television in the living-room. Ben edged the bedclothes over his nose. The air was cooler and fresher than underneath the sheets. He knew Max was there at the side of the bed. Though he could not hear or see him, he still knew he was there.

'Max,' he whispered in a strangled voice. Max did not reply.

'I'm going to put the light on, Max.' He tried to put a threat into the words but they came out feebly. With his heart thumping he felt for the edge of the bed. The floor was cold on his feet. He stood up and groped in front of him. Max wasn't there. Ben strained his eyes. Though he could not see a thing he knew, if he kept walking he would come to the door.

He was about to move again when a floorboard squeaked behind him. Ben swung round.

'Max. Max, is that you?' he called out hoarsely. His throat was dry and he could hardly speak.

'I am the ghost of the mine.' The voice came from by the bed, a high-pitched voice like the croaking of a raven. Ben knew it was Max. Max could imitate all sorts of people when he wanted to. 'I am the ghost of the mine,' the voice repeated, 'I have come to haunt you. Ha-ha-ha-ha.' It was a horrible laugh.

It was Max. He knew it was Max.

'Come to the mine. Come to the mine or I will return and haunt you.' There was a scuffle near the bed. It was Max. It was.

Ben stumbled forward in terror. The light switch couldn't be far away. He reached the wall and felt around on the scratchy, plaster surface. At last he found the square, plastic fitting. He fumbled and brought the switch down with his trembling hand.

The bright light dazzled him. He covered his eyes with one arm. For a few moments he could not see a thing. Then the brightness faded. Max was lying in bed, the clothes over his head, his face to the wall. He was making loud breathing noises through his nose, the way some people do when they are asleep.

'You think you're very clever,' Ben said almost in tears. Max didn't answer. He went on breathing through his nose.

'I'm going to tell Mum if you won't wake up,' Ben told him. Ben waited and waited but Max ignored him.

'All right, I'm going,' Ben said finally. He opened the door and went through the hall into the living-room.

Mum was sitting in her armchair watching the television, her hands moving quickly as she knitted.

'Mum,' Ben whimpered, 'Max is frightening me and he won't let me go to sleep.'

Mum looked at Ben. He was a sad, small figure shivering in the doorway. The cord on his striped pyjamas was undone. Mum sighed, placed her knitting on the floor, grasped the arms of the chair and pulled herself up with great effort.

'You are naughty boys,' she said in a complaining tone. 'You should have been asleep hours ago.' She followed Ben through to the bedroom.

Max was in exactly the same position, still making the loud breathing noises through his nose.

'Max,' Mum said sharply. She took hold of his shoulder and shook him hard. Max sat up suddenly, put his hands to his eyes, yawned and gazed around him as though he couldn't understand where he was.

'What! What is it?' he exclaimed in a loud voice.

'You've been upsetting Ben again,' she said angrily. Max shook his head in astonishment. He pointed a finger at his chest.

'Me, Mum! I've been asleep. I don't know what you're talking about.'

'Don't you be cheeky with me, my boy,' she told him. 'Now both of you into bed, and I don't want to hear a word from either of you.'

She let go of Ben's hand. He went over to the chair, clutched his Teddy-bear in his arms and climbed into bed.

'Mum,' Ben said softly, as she was about to switch off the light, 'Max promised I could sleep by the wall tonight.'

Max half-closed his eyes, fury written on his face. He looked appealingly at Mum. 'If you promised, Max, you promised,' she said. Max opened his mouth to speak, and then decided not to. He slid over to the outside of the bed, pulling the clothes with him. Ben clambered on top of him, and rolled the Teddy-bear so that it squeaked in Max's ear.

The light went off. The door shut. Max and Ben lay like frightened mice until they heard the armchair creak as Mum sat down in it. 'You big baby,' Max whispered.

'It was you. You needn't think I didn't know,' Ben told him, spitting through his teeth.

'You wake me up once more and I'll break your little neck,' Max said savagely. He turned away from Ben, taking the sheets with him. Then he began his breathing noises again.

'He's a liar. He was the ghost,' Ben whispered to himself loud enough for Max to hear. 'I'm not speaking to him. He'll be sorry. One day he'll be sorry.'

Later when Ben was almost asleep the clothes slipped from his body. He awoke with a start, shivering from the cold. He leaned over Max and heaved with all his might, but Max wouldn't let go. Ben kicked him in the back and pulled again. Still Max held on. 'I'll tell Mum,' Ben warned. Max's grip on the bedclothes loosened.

'Needn't think he can bully me,' Ben said, settling down near the wall. 'If he tries one more thing I'm going straight to Mum.' Max snorted through his nose and rolled over quickly, squashing the breath out of Ben's body. Then he gave Ben the kick he owed him. Ben was thinking of his revenge when the door silently opened. The shaft of light lit up Mum's face. She stood there for several moments, listening, before she went into her own bedroom.

Max and Ben knew they would have to be quiet now, for Mum could hear the slightest sound they made from her own room. 'Truce,' Max whispered. He gave Ben's shoulder a friendly squeeze. Not long after that they were fast asleep.

CHAPTER TWO

Parcel from Australia

THE SUN rose slowly above the slackheaps. At first they appeared black and sinister, but as the sun climbed higher they were suffused with light that transformed them to a dull grey colour. The sun was behind the mine making it stand out sharply against the bright pearl sky. The air was cold and a heavy dampness hung over the heaps from the morning dew. At this time of day it seemed even stiller than usual, and the seven-thirty train, which clattered past, lit up the landscape with noise. The ground shook for a few seconds, the train droned away into the distance, then the silence returned.

The two brothers heard the train from their room. Max clambered out of bed and walked to the window. The sun shone into his eyes. He looked at the mass of weeds and long grass in the back garden. Dad had turned over the soil when he had last been home on leave, but the weeds quickly returned, and now it was as overgrown as when they had first moved into the house. Max had promised Dad he would keep the garden tidy, but the soil was mostly clay and it was too hard for Max to work. Max felt a pang of guilt. But it did not last long. He had come to the window to see the mine. He did not know why, but the sight of the chimney-stack excited him. It drew him towards it. For some reason, which he could not explain to himself, he knew he would have to go there again.

Ben pulled the curtain aside and climbed on to the chair. Perhaps it was on account of Ben, because Ben was so afraid of the mine. When they were on the slackheaps Max knew he was infinitely stronger than his brother.

Neither of them spoke of their quarrel of the previous evening. After a time they went through into the living-room. The Sunday papers lay scattered on the floor and the stale smell of Mum's cigarettes hung in the air. The curtains were drawn. The room was cool and in half-darkness.

'My feet are cold. Go and fetch my slippers,' Max ordered, 'I'll make the tea.' Ben didn't like being told what to do, but he did it because he wasn't allowed to make the tea, and while Max had the excuse of being busy, Ben couldn't refuse.

When he returned Max had put out three cups and the electric kettle had begun to sing as it heated. Max took the slippers from Ben without saying thank you.

'You can take Mum's cup,' he said. Ben didn't object. It was a job he liked. Mum had her tea in bed every morning when they were on holiday.

Steam rose to the ceiling as Max switched off the kettle and poured the water into the teapot.

'Stir it three times for luck,' Max mumbled, as if he was casting a spell. He wiped a speck of dust from Mum's cup and then poured in the tea.

Ben took the saucer with both hands and pulled back the kitchen door with his foot. Not for one instant did he take his eyes from the level of the tea in the cup. Mum sat up in bed as he opened her door. She brushed her hair from her face, turned over the counterpane and straightened the sheets. Ben held out the tea with trembling hands. Then he sat on the edge of the bed and watched her drink it.

'Thank you, Ben,' she said. 'I suppose I ought to be making your breakfast for you.' Ben didn't answer. He was looking at the assortment of perfumes, lipstick, powder and brushes which were scattered on the dressing-table. Altogether they gave the room a sweet, musty smell.

'Open the window, Ben, there's a good boy,' Mum said, as if she had read his thoughts.

Ben moved the chair with her clothes on it and climbed up. Fresh, cold air came through the window. There was the distant hum of the town a long way away.

'Now be off with you, Benny,' she told him, 'and

then I can dress myself.' Ben picked up her cup and went back into the living-room.

Max was sitting by the window gazing out into the street. 'Mum says you have to make our bed,' Ben told him. Max grunted but he didn't move. Ben sat next to him on the low window ledge. The front lawn bristled with dew, and there were patches of wetness on the black tar road and the square, white stones of the pavement. The curtains were drawn in all the front windows except theirs. Max stood up and went to their room. Ben followed him and they both dressed. He waited to see whether Max would make the bed but he didn't so Ben made it himself. Then they went back to the kitchen.

Mum had the table laid. She was standing by the stove stirring the porridge in a saucepan.

'Just in time, you two,' she said. They sat at the table and Mum poured the porridge into their bowls. It was hot and some of it stuck to the saucepan. Mum scraped it out with the wooden spoon. Steam rose from the bowls. Max blew on his, made a hole in the middle and then poured milk in. He reached over Ben's plate and took the sugar bowl.

'Where're your manners?' Mum said sharply.

'Excuse me, Benjamin,' Max said, in a polite voice which was really meant to be sarcastic.

'And that sugar has to last till tomorrow,' she told him, as Max ladled two heapfuls on to his porridge. She took the sugar off him and sprinkled one small spoonful over Ben's bowl.

Then she switched on the transistor radio above the sink. There was a low humming noise and then a voice came on, 'Mrs Hill of King Street, Aberdeen. This is your record.' It was 'Housewife's Choice'. A man began singing, 'I lost my heart in an English garden.' Mum turned the volume control down and remembered the toast. She lifted the slices quickly with the ends of her fingers and dropped them into the toast-rack on the table. She knocked up the switch on the stove, poured out the tea and sat next to Ben at the table. She watched him spreading marmalade thickly on his toast as she lit a cigarette. She blew smoke through her nose. It whirled in ever-changing patterns about the room.

Max put the last piece of toast into his mouth and said, 'Please may I leave the table?' Hardly before Mum had answered him he was out through the door. The postman was on the other side of the street. Max sat on the stone wall, scraping his nails, his heart beating quickly.

The postman crossed the road, sorting letters in his hand. He walked straight past Max. Max sighed, ambled up the path and into the kitchen again.

'What are you looking so glum for?' Mum asked as he came in.

'The postman's just been and Dad's parcel hasn't arrived,' Max explained despondently.

'Well, never mind,' Mum told him, 'there's another delivery at half-past eleven and the parcel van comes in the morning as well. If it's a really large parcel the

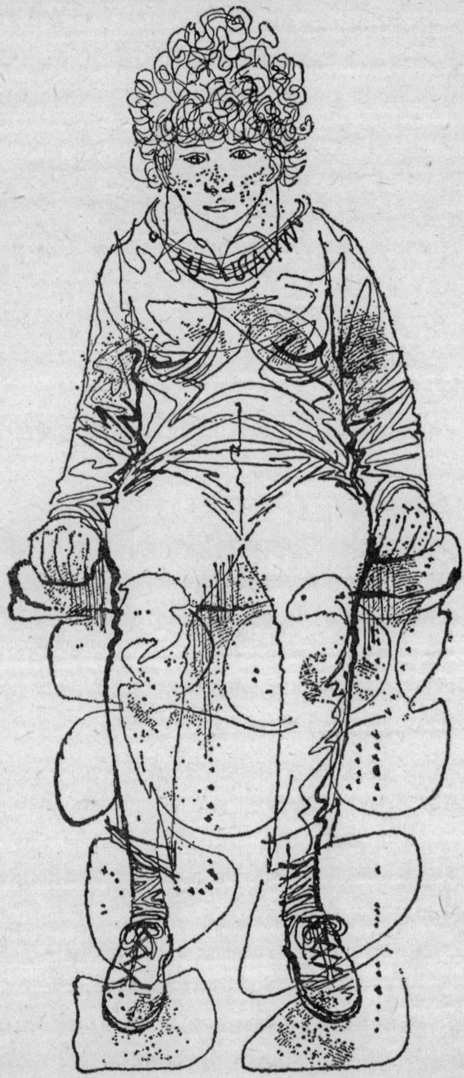

postman wouldn't be able to carry it in his bag.'

What she said turned out to be correct, because an hour later the red van came slowly along their street. The driver was looking out of his cab at the numbers on the doors. He stopped outside their house.

'It's Dad's parcel,' Ben shouted excitedly. Mum lifted her dripping hands from the sink. She reached out for the drying-up cloth and wiped her hands with it.

'Won't be a moment,' she called, as there was a knock at the door.

'Morning, ma'am,' the delivery man called through the window.

'Good morning,' Mum replied, opening the door for him, 'Would you bring it into the living-room, please.' He strode across the step, leaving a trail of black footsteps behind him on the linoleum. Mum didn't shout or say anything to him. He lowered the parcel on to the table but he let go too soon and it thumped down, causing everything inside to rattle and shake. Mum came from the kitchen and wrote her name in the little book the delivery man produced from his tunic pocket.

'Would you like a cup of tea?' Mum asked.

'No, thank you very much, ma'am,' he said, 'very kind of you, but I won't stay now.'

Mum showed him out by the kitchen door. He raised his cap to her, climbed in his van and drove off. When she came back into the room, the breadknife in one hand, Mum found Max and Ben having a tug of war with the parcel between them. They did not hear her come in and the first thing they saw was the breadknife flashing in front of their eyes. They both let go at once. The parcel fell with a thump on the table. Max and Ben collapsed in untidy heaps on the floor. Mum raised the knife above her head as if she was going to strike. They instinctively closed their eyes as a wave of fear went through their bodies. 'You two,' Mum said, 'I'll skin you alive one day.' Max and Ben exchanged glances and grinned.

'May I cut the string?' Ben pleaded.

'No. He did it last year,' Max complained.

'I'll do it myself and then there'll be no argument,' Mum told them.

They watched her hands as she slashed the knots one by one. Max pushed away the loose string. Mum laid the knife on the table. The three of them turned the parcel over. The brown paper was held down with Sellotape. Max and Ben goggled at the rows of foreign stamps, franked over and over with black registration marks.

'That's mine,' Max said pointing at one.

'And I'm having this one,' Ben shouted excitedly.

Mum pushed them aside, slit the brown paper with the knife and began tearing it off in strips.

'Be careful, the stamps,' Max cried, picking each piece of paper up as it fell to the floor.

Soon it was all off. What remained was a large cardboard cigarette box. It was held together with thick, hairy, white string. Max joggled the box from side to side, rattling it to see if he could guess from the sounds what was inside. Mum cut the string. It broke with a snappy twang. They all crowded round the box. Mum pulled open the lid and they stared in. There was soft, coloured paper, the kind oranges are wrapped with. Max tore it away. Beneath was the first present. It was a pale blue night-dress with large red roses over it. Mum held it against herself and asked them whether it was nice. But Max and Ben did not answer. They had returned to the parcel. There was more wrapping paper, and then next came Max's present. It was in a long flat box. Ben looked over his shoulder as he took it out. There was a picture of an aeroplane on the outside, the sort of aeroplane which landed on Dad's ship. Inside the box were a number of pieces of wood, coloured transfers and a tube of glue.

'Read what the letter says,' Mum said. Max took out a square piece of blue paper which was lodged in the lid of the box. 'This is for you, Max,' he read, 'I hope you are able to make it yourself. It won't be long before I am home now. Love, Dad. P.S. It really will fly.'

'Now yours, Ben,' Mum said, giving him a nudge. Ben had been lost for an instant staring at Max's present. If only the aeroplane had been for him. He knew his present wouldn't be as good as Max's. Max always had the best of everything.

The box was half empty and Ben had to reach far down before his hands closed over something square. It was heavy, a book perhaps, it felt like a book. He didn't want a book, he wanted an aeroplane. He lifted the present up and pulled off the wrapping paper. It wasn't exactly a book. It was a stamp album. There were pictures of different flags on the front, and on the inside Dad had stuck stamps here and there, one from Singapore, three from Hong Kong and a lot from Australia.

'It's nice, isn't it, Mum?' Ben said. He knew it would please her if he showed he liked it. Mum beamed at him.

'You've forgotten the rest of the parcel,' she reminded them. And they had too. Below another layer of orange papers there was a bottle of perfume for Mum and there were all sorts of sweets for Max and Ben.

When they reached the bottom of the box Mum picked up her night-dress and perfume and went to her bedroom. Max laid the parts of his aeroplane on the carpet. Ben piled all the sweets together in one big heap. He separated the chocolate ones out for himself and gave all the toffees to Max.

'Thanks, Ben,' Max said cheerfully, undoing one of the wrappers and stuffing the sweet into his mouth without looking at it. He was in a good mood. He also knew he had the best present.

Mum came back in the room, a quiet smile on her face. She said she wanted to vacuum the carpet. Max clucked to himself, put all the pieces on the lid of the box and carried them to his bed. Soon the wings were fitted, then the tail was slotted in. The room was filled with the smell of glue, lacquer and green paint which Max applied with a tiny brush. Finally he pulled the

paper backing from the transfers, wet them with his tongue and pressed them to the wings and body of the aeroplane.

Max stood up, and held the plane away from him to admire it. Ben watched him, bitter with envy.

'Let's see if she will fly,' Max said, grinning happily. Ben tried to smile back at him but he found it very difficult.

'Where are you off to?' Mum wanted to know as they tried to creep out of the door without being seen.

'We're only going to fly my aeroplane,' Max explained.

'Well, don't be long, because dinner will be ready in five minutes.'

'We won't,' Max agreed.

Ben followed Max out into the middle of the street. Max stretched the elastic along the undercarriage, he pointed the nose to the sky and then let go. The aeroplane soared upwards, far higher than Max thought it would. It seemed to hover in mid-air as birds do, then it glided gracefully down and grated along the road. Max and Ben chased after it. The paint was slightly scratched but it was nothing very much.

'Let me have a try,' Ben pleaded.

'Just once,' Max said, 'but be careful it doesn't go in a garden. If old Johns gets it he'll never give us it back. This afternoon we'll take it to the slackheaps. There'll be no danger there.'

Ben took the aeroplane from him. It was big in his

hands. When he stretched the elastic it sprang off, stinging his fingers.

'Not like that, fool,' Max told him. 'Keep it straight, like this.' Ben held the plane firmly and tried again. He stretched the elastic tight. Then without meaning to he let go. The aeroplane careered wildly in circles. Max and Ben started after it. They did not notice the man on a bike as he came round the corner. They ran towards the aeroplane as it came down. The man jammed on his brakes and tinkled the bell. Max and Ben stopped just in time. The bike halted suddenly as the plane skidded on to the road.

It was Mr Mansion the policeman. He lived two houses away from Max and Ben. He dismounted from his bike and picked up the aeroplane. Fortunately it wasn't broken.

'And who gave you this?' he asked kindly.

'It's Max's,' Ben told him. 'Dad sent it to him from Australia.'

'And what did he send for you, Ben?'

'I've got a stamp album, but it's in the house.'

'Is that so?' Mr Mansion said with a smile.

'Yes,' Ben told him. 'Shall I fetch it for you?'

'No, not now, Ben. It's time for my dinner. You bring it to my house this afternoon and Max can come as well if he wants to.'

He waved good-bye to them, wheeled his bike along the pavement and disappeared into his driveway.

'Do you know what?' Ben said as Mum served out the soup. 'We're going to Mr Mansion's house this afternoon and he wants to look at my stamp album.'

'You can go,' Max said grumpily, 'but I'm not coming.' He ate his dinner without saying a word. When he had finished he picked up his aeroplane and went out of the door.

CHAPTER THREE

The Ship

BEN KNEW why Max was annoyed. Max was afraid of Mr Mansion. Perhaps it was because he was a policeman. At all events he was embarrassed whenever Mr Mansion talked to him, and he would not go to the policeman's house. Now he had gone to the slackheaps on his own. Ben felt a tinge of jealousy, as he did when Max went anywhere without him. But this afternoon there was the compensation of seeing Mr Mansion.

'You had better wait for a few minutes,' Mum told him, 'I'm sure Mr Mansion would like a little rest. He's been working since five o'clock this morning.'

'All right,' Ben said. 'Do you know where there are any old pieces of wood?'

'And what do you want wood for?' Mum asked him severely.

'I'm going to make a ship, and if Mr Mansion isn't busy he might help me with it.'

'Now Ben, Mr Mansion has too much to do. I don't want you to bother him.'

'Then I'll make it myself,' Ben said in a peevish voice.

Mum didn't answer him. Ben nearly asked her again about the wood but he thought better of it. Instead he cleared the dirty dishes and put them in the sink. He turned on the hot tap and sprinkled a few drops of washing-up liquid into the water. He was careful not to squeeze out too much. He took one of the stools from under the table and placed it by the sink. He enjoyed washing dishes, especially when Max wasn't there. Max sneered at him for doing it and called him 'Little toady'. Max said he was only trying to get on the right side of Mum, but whether that was true or not washing dishes never failed to put her in a good humour.

When he had finished Mum gave him a kiss, let him have a drink of orange juice, and said there were lots of old pieces of wood in the garage. Ben skipped along the drive. He jumped up and touched the washing-line as he went past it. The garage door wasn't locked. Dad had lost the key when he had last been home on leave. Ben heaved open the heavy door. Cobwebs stretched between the rafters. There was just enough room for Ben to squeeze past the car. The roof and windows were clouded with dust. Nobody had been in the garage since the last night of Dad's leave when he had taken them to the pictures.

Ben found two pieces of wood in Dad's toolbox. He borrowed Dad's saw and hammer. Dad wouldn't mind, not when Ben explained he had been building a ship.

Mum refused to allow him into the house so Ben made the ship on the door-step. It wasn't nearly so easy as he had expected it to be. The saw wouldn't cut straight. It slipped and tore a jagged line on his thumb, which filled with blood.

Still Ben managed to make a ship. It didn't exactly look like a ship, but that is what Ben had meant it to be. He brushed away the sawdust from the door and then he asked Mum if he could go.

'Yes. You can go. But remember what I said about asking Mr Mansion to make anything for you.'

'I won't forget,' Ben promised. He left her sitting in her armchair, knitting and listening to 'Woman's Hour' on the radio.

Mr Mansion was in the shed at the bottom of his garden. He nearly always worked there when he was at home. He built the shed himself last year. Ben watched him do it. That was how Ben came to know him. He had seen the policeman before that time, controlling the traffic on the main road which led into town. Like Max, Ben had been frightened of him to begin with. Mr Mansion was such a tall man, taller than anybody else the brothers knew. Every time he went through a door he had to lower his head. His hair was jet black except for a few strands of grey and there was a blue-black patch round his chin where he shaved. From a distance he was like any other policeman. It was when he had built the shed that Ben found him to be different. Max and Ben had watched him one Saturday afternoon wheeling barrow-loads of sand to the end of his garden.

'Let's go and see what he's doing,' Ben had suggested. Max refused, so Ben went on his own. He stood outside the policeman's house, where sand was piled high on the pavement.

'And what can we do for you?' Mr Mansion had asked with a twinkle in his eye. Ben liked him immediately. He liked the way his mouth curled up when he smiled and the tiny wrinkles which appeared under his eyes whenever he spoke. That first day his face had been covered with perspiration and he was breathing hard.

'May I watch you?' Ben had said shyly.

'Of course you can watch,' Mr Mansion told him with a laugh. 'There's no law against watching.'

Ben walked down the path of broken stones. On either side there were neat rows of vegetables and flowers.

The shed was made from cedar wood. Mr Mansion had painted it with creosote to prevent it from rotting. Ben pushed the stamp album and ship under his jersey. He hesitated outside the door and listened. There wasn't a sound, but Ben knew Mr Mansion was inside. He knocked softly and looked up at the clear afternoon sky. There was a coldness in the air which is often there at the end of the summer holidays.

For an instant Ben thought about Max flying his aeroplane on the slackheaps near the mine. Then there was a cough and the sound of somebody standing up from a chair. Ben turned back to the door as it opened.

'Come in,' Mr Mansion said in a loud friendly voice. He was wearing his brown overalls. Ben could see his policeman's blue shirt underneath.

Ben went into the hut. It was like entering another world; it was as though the houses outside had ceased to exist. The walls were lined with shelves and on them stood tins and bottles. Tins of paint, tins of varnish, jamjars and bottles with screws and nails inside them. Above the shelves, supported on hooks, hung saws, hammers, chisels and planes. In one corner was the workbench, and by its side was an old chair with a straw seat which sagged when it was sat on. The floor was covered with sawdust and wood chippings, and in the hut there was a beautiful smell, not one smell but a mixture of wood, creosote, paint and varnish.

Mr Mansion had a small box in his hand. It was hardly any larger than a matchbox. It was made from a dark, red wood, the colour of copperbeech leaves, and there were neat, perfect-fitting joints at each corner.

'What is it?' Ben exclaimed with admiration. Mr Mansion gave it to him to hold. Ben turned it over in his hand. Then he lifted the tiny lid and looked inside.

'It's a trinket-box. I made it for a niece of mine. It's her birthday next week,' Mr Mansion explained.

'Isn't it beautiful,' was all Ben could think of to say.

'Careful now,' Mr Mansion said. 'Mind you don't

mark it with your fingers.' Mr Mansion took the box from Ben and laid it gently on the workbench.

'You can watch me varnish it,' Mr Mansion told Ben.

Underneath the shelves there were three drawers. From one of them Mr Mansion took a brush. He wiped it clean on a piece of cloth and stropped it across the back of his hand. Then he undid a bottle of varnish and poured a little of it into a saucer. Ben watched his fingers turning over the box as he painted it. The wood darkened as the brush was drawn across it. A fly circled round the bare electric light bulb above their heads. Otherwise, except for their breathing, the room was motionless and still.

It did not take long. When it was finished Mr Mansion dropped the brush into a jar of turps and placed the box back on the bench. He sat down in the chair and looked at Ben, a smile playing on his face.

'And what have we there?' he asked suddenly, reaching out and digging Ben in the ribs with his long fingers. Ben pulled out the stamp album and the ship from under his jumper, and handed them to Mr Mansion. He waited apprehensively. After seeing the box, Ben now felt ashamed of the ship.

Mr Mansion placed the ship on his knee as if he hadn't noticed it. He picked up the stamp album and held it to the light. 'This looks very good,' he said softly as he turned the pages.

'Those are Australian stamps,' Ben explained, 'that's where Dad was when he bought the book for me.'

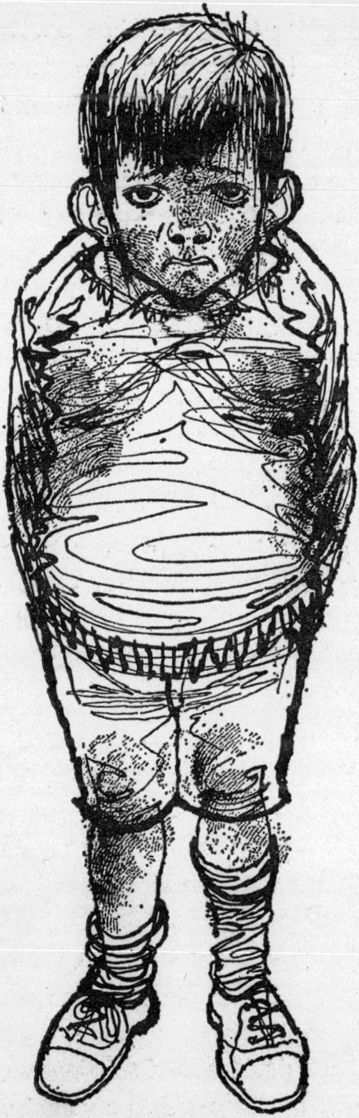

'I understand,' Mr Mansion said. He went on examining the album, lifting up the stamps and peering underneath them.

'You're a very lucky boy,' he said as he handed the stamp album to Ben.

'And what is this?' he asked, taking the ship off his knee.

'It's a—it's a—' Ben said, but he couldn't manage to say the word ship. Tears welled into his eyes. He sniffed loudly and wiped his eyes with his hand. Mr Mansion did not speak. He only looked into Ben's face with that kind expression of understanding. And then Ben was ashamed of crying. It was stupid to cry. Mr Mansion wouldn't laugh at him.

'Did you make it?' Mr Mansion asked in that soft voice of his. Ben nodded. He took out his handkerchief and blew loudly through his nose. Then he found his voice.

'It's all because of Max,' Ben said sobbing, 'Dad sent Max an aeroplane and that's what I wanted but I haven't got one.'

'But this isn't an aeroplane, Ben,' Mr Mansion said, looking puzzled.

'No, it's a ship. I wanted to make a ship like the one Dad sails in but it doesn't look like it at all. I can never do anything properly. I've tried but I can't.'

'One day you will, though. When you grow up you'll be better than me. You wait and see.'

'But I want a ship like Dad's now,' Ben said. And without meaning to he started to cry again.

'Then if you want a ship now, we'll make it together,' Mr Mansion said cheerfully. Ben drew in his breath. He didn't know what to say. Really this was what he had hoped for. He had thought that morning, 'Mr Mansion will make a ship better than Max's aeroplane.' But in his heart he had not expected it to happen. 'You run home, Ben, and bring me the picture of your Dad's ship, and I'll find the wood we need.' Ben nodded through his tears. Mr Mansion opened the door for him and he went out into the cold, hard September afternoon.

The sky had clouded over and there was a light rain, the kind of rain which makes one look up to see if one has been mistaken. This time it was rain. Tiny drops sprinkled down on Ben's face, touching his skin like little cold fingers.

Mum was in the back garden taking in the washing. Mrs Johns was talking to her across the fence. Mum didn't see Ben. He was glad she didn't. If she found out Mr Mansion was helping him with the ship she might make him stay in. Ben raced through the kitchen and lounge, banging the doors in excitement as he went. The picture came off the wall without any difficulty. He folded it twice and slipped it into his pocket.

Mum was still talking to Mrs Johns when he opened the door. He waited till her head was turned and then ran down the drive and out of sight.

Mr Mansion had switched on the small electric wall fire and the air in the hut was soft and warm.

'You never had time to find it?' Mr Mansion said, 'I

haven't had a chance to say "Jack Robinson" since you've been away.' Ben pulled the crumpled picture out of his pocket and eagerly thrust it into Mr Mansion's hands. He knew there would be little he would be able to do to help make the ship, but the picture was his and he was proud of it.

'Thank you, Ben,' Mr Mansion said. He stood for a long time, one hand cupped to his chin, an expression of deep thought on his face. Ben watched him, afraid to make any sound or movement, in case he might spoil what was in Mr Mansion's mind.

'Yes, I know,' Mr Mansion finally said. He propped the picture against the back of the chair.

'There, now we can see what we are doing,' he said. He reached under the workbench and found a piece of wood. It was white and clean with grain marks running along it. In Mr Mansion's hand it seemed minute but really it was almost the size of a brick. From one of the drawers Mr Mansion took a knife. He held the wood firmly in one hand and pared at it with the sharp blade. Shavings flew away in all directions as if the wood had been butter.

Ben reached up on tiptoe. Before his eyes the wood changed into the shape of a ship. It was the most wonderful sight he had ever seen. The knife moved rapidly, first one way then another way. The white shavings piled up on the floor beneath their feet. Not once did Mr Mansion's eyes move away from the wood. Ben expected the policeman to say the ship was finished but he didn't. And as each minute passed the ship came more and more to resemble the picture propped against the chair.

Ben longed to express his admiration, to say something at least. But Mr Mansion's heavy breathing and the manner in which his hands moved somehow commanded Ben to silence.

Then at last it was finished: Mr Mansion held the ship above his head as if trying to decide whether anything more was needed.

'That'll do it, don't you think, Ben?'

'It's just like the picture,' Ben said quietly. He lifted his hands to try and touch the ship.

'Yes, that's right. You see for yourself,' said Mr Mansion.

Ben took the model with both hands. Was it really going to be his? Mr Mansion had said so. Yet it was too good for a toy, much better than anything Ben had ever owned before. What would Max say when he saw it? He'd want to swop it for his aeroplane. Ben bit his lip.

'Is it mine now?' he asked. It took all Ben's courage to ask the question, and when he did so he looked away from the policeman and stared at the shavings on the floor.

'Of course it's yours,' Mr Mansion said with a laugh. 'It's yours if you would like to have it.'

'It's perfect,' Ben said. He wanted to say a lot more, to thank Mr Mansion over and over, but he could not think how to put it into words so he said nothing. He felt shy now, and more than anything he wanted to go home and show the ship to Max and Mum. All the toys he had ever owned had been old or had once belonged to Max, and because of this they had made him feel only second-best himself. But the ship was different. The ship was better than a toy. Already Ben felt the ship was part of himself.

'Mind you, we haven't painted her yet,' Mr Mansion said, 'and we don't know for certain whether she'll float or not. A boat would be no good if she didn't float.'

Ben's face fell. It would mean he wouldn't be able to take the ship with him tonight.

'Now, don't you worry,' Mr Mansion said, seeing Ben's disappointment, 'I'll paint her right away and then you can float her in your bath, and if she capsizes you can bring her back to me tomorrow.'

Ben heaved a sigh of relief. Mr Mansion lifted two small tins of paint down from the shelf. He squeezed the wet out of the brush, the same brush he had used to paint the trinket box.

'I'm afraid I haven't the colours of your father's ship,' Mr Mansion said, 'but I could probably buy them in town tomorrow.'

'It doesn't matter,' Ben said, his voice full of anxiety, 'any colour will do.' He could not bear the possibility of the ship not being finished.

'There's red and blue. Now will they be all right?' Mr Mansion asked. Ben nodded without speaking.

'Well, how would you like to finish her off for yourself,' Mr Mansion said, holding the brush out towards Ben. Ben shrank back against the wall as if he was frightened the brush was going to hurt him.

'Oh! No, you finish it please,' he said. He knew if he had any part of the making of the ship, then it might be ruined.

Mr Mansion smiled to himself. He prised the lids open with the end of a screwdriver. The smell of paint filled the hut. Mr Mansion carefully painted the funnels and the mast red. The remainder he did in blue. For a few seconds after the paint had been applied it glistened on the surface of the wood, catching the light from the bare bulb. Then the wetness disappeared, soaking into the pores of the wood. Mr Mansion held the ship by the middle mast. When he had painted up to his fingers he balanced the hull on the palm of his hand and painted the tiny patch of bare wood which remained.

'There we are, Ben,' Mr Mansion said. 'Hold her very lightly till the paint dries. And remember, if she doesn't float properly you bring her back tomorrow afternoon.'

'Thank you. Thank you very much for making it for me. It was very kind of you.' Ben spoke the words slowly and clearly. He knew that was what he ought to say, but it did not express the gratitude he felt towards the policeman.

'Think nothing of it,' Mr Mansion said. He opened the door and held it for Ben. He fumbled in his pockets for a bunch of keys. He glanced round the shed, switched off the light and then locked the door behind him.

The clouds were low in the sky. A wind had blown up. It was going to rain heavily soon.

'Don't wait for me,' Mr Mansion called, 'you don't want to get your boat wet before she's properly dried.' Ben turned and waved and then he ran down Mr Mansion's driveway. The wind came in great gusts between the houses. It caught Ben off balance and nearly blew him off his feet. Ben clutched the ship tightly and walked backwards. By doing this he seemed to be walking through a tunnel where there was no wind. It howled all around him, coming suddenly and then dying down again only to return stronger a few seconds later.

The curtains were not drawn in the front room. Max was lying on the carpet in front of the fire watching television. Ben tiptoed past the window. Max didn't see him. The kitchen door was open. Mum was outside pouring tea leaves down the drain. 'My goodness me. You gave me a shock,' she said, as she straightened with the teapot in her hand.

'Don't touch it, it's not properly dry yet,' Ben told her. He hurried past her into the living-room. She gave him a peculiar look, the sort of look which meant he had done something wrong. Max didn't take his eyes off the television set when Ben came in. There was a scowl on his face. Ben could tell he was in a bad mood. Ben took the ship into his bedroom and put it on the window-ledge. He stood admiring it for a long time, thinking only of the ship and what he would do with it. Then there was a scuffle. When he turned Max was standing behind him staring at the ship through half-closed eyes. Ben knew he wasn't very pleased.

Then Mum called that tea was on the table and it was going cold. Max sat down opposite Ben and stirred his tea noisily. He picked a scone up and took a huge bite out of it. Before Mum saw him he stuffed the rest of it into his mouth. He moved his jaws very slowly so as not to make a noise. He managed to swallow half of it, then Mum turned round from the stove. She took the cigarette out of her mouth and stared into Max's face. 'What's in your mouth?' she asked him angrily. Max swallowed frantically. He coughed violently as if he was in a fit. Crumbs flew across the room. Some of them went in Ben's hair.

'What are you eating?' Mum shouted.

'Nothing,' Max lied. Mum grasped hold of his head and forced his jaws apart. Ben could see the pink of Max's throat. His mouth was full of chewed-up scone.

'Don't you tell lies to me, my boy,' Mum told him angrily, 'and you needn't smile on the side of your face, Benjamin, because it doesn't seem funny to me.'

After that nobody said a word. Mum dished out the beans and sausages and they sat round the table in silence. The only sounds were their munching mouths and the clink of knives and forks. As soon as they had finished, Max and Ben excused themselves and escaped to their bedroom. Max threw himself on the bed and stared at the ceiling. Ben had never seen him looking so depressed.

Ben walked to the window-ledge and picked up the ship. The paint was dry now. He went into the bathroom and ran the cold water in the bath. He leaned over and fitted the plug in the hole. He waited, watching the water swirl around and around. When the bath was a quarter full Ben turned off the tap. He lowered the ship gently. It sank under the surface, then it bobbed up again. It floated perfectly upright. Ben knew it would. Everything Mr Mansion made was perfect. Ben pushed the ship along the bath. It knocked against the side, turned and floated in the opposite direction. He played for five minutes, his mind imagining how the ship would look on the lake near the slackheaps. Then Mum shouted from the living-room that it was nearly time for bed. Ben lifted the ship out of the bath and dried it with the towel from the rail on the door.

Max hadn't moved. He was still lying in the same position on the bed. Ben put the ship on the window-ledge. He waited for Max to speak, at least to ask him

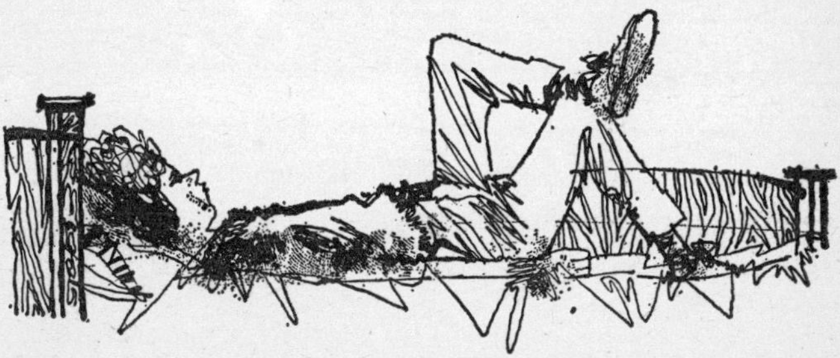

where the ship had come from, but when Max said nothing, Ben knew there was something wrong. He sat on the edge of the bed, uncertain whether he should take his brother's hand or not.

'What's the matter, Max?' Ben asked.

'I've lost my aeroplane,' Max said in a thick voice. Ben couldn't think what to say.

'It fell down the mineshaft, I was flying it across the slackheaps and it went down the hole.' Ben tried to look sympathetic. He really did feel sorry, but the feeling was mingled with a certain pleasure, pleasure that Max had lost his aeroplane while he had the ship.

'There's a ladder by the side of the hole,' Max was saying, 'I saw it this afternoon. Tomorrow I'm going to take Dad's torch and with some rope I'll climb down the shaft.'

Ben nearly said Max might fall, but he knew if he did Max would call him a baby. So he pretended he thought nothing of it. He shrugged his shoulders and walked to the door.

'If you tell Mum I'll kill you,' Max told him.

'Don't worry, I won't,' Ben answered. He left Max lying on the bed and went into the living-room and watched television until Mum made him turn it off.

Max eyed him suspiciously when they were cleaning their teeth in the bathroom.

'I haven't said a word,' Ben said. Max looked into his eyes to see if he was speaking the truth.

'Honestly, I didn't,' Ben added, trying to put conviction into his voice. Max grunted and slammed the door behind him. Ben washed his face and had a drink of water. Afterwards he kissed Mum goodnight. Max used to when he was small, but after he left the Infant School he said kissing was only for babies and girls.

When Ben opened the bedroom door the room was in darkness. Ben felt for the switch and pressed it down. He walked over to the window-ledge and picked up the ship. It was the best ship in the world. Max sat up, pushed the sheets away from his face and glared at Ben. He glanced at the ship and then rolled over to the wall.

'Turn off the light,' he ordered, 'I want to go to sleep.'

Why should I, thought Ben, he doesn't let me sleep

when I want to. He pretended to play with the ship, he floated it in the air and made the sound of waves with his lips. But when Max didn't start an argument he decided to go to bed himself. He laid the ship on the floor by his bed, stepped out of his slippers and switched off the light.

But he couldn't fall asleep. He lay and listened to the television in the front room and to the occasional cars which droned past. He waited for Max to wake up but Max didn't move. In a certain way he was disappointed. He always lost the fights with Max but without them there was a feeling of emptiness. He trailed his hand beside the bed and felt for the ship. He lifted it up and dragged it under the sheets. The ship was his and nobody would ever be able to take it away from him. Once he thought of Max's aeroplane at the bottom of the mine, but it was only once.

CHAPTER FOUR

A Matter of Life and Death

IT RAINED in the night. Huge drops cascaded on to the garage roof. The dull pattering sound woke Max up. His heart sank when he heard the noise. If it was raining in the morning it would not be possible to go to the mine for Mum would make them stay indoors. For an hour it went on relentlessly and then gradually the pattering quietened. Max listened for a while. Later he drifted back into sleep.

But the rain hadn't ceased. It had changed to a fine drizzle, enveloping everything in mist. The deafening noise of the early trains was muffled by the wetness all around. The windows were clouded over from the hot air and the cigarette smoke. For the people on their way to town, the mine did not exist that morning.

But the mine was there, its red brickwork streaked and darkened by the rain. Water hung from the doorway, dripping continually on to the heavy coaldust below. During the night a visitor had arrived on the slackheaps. He was a tramp, caught by the downpour while walking along the railway embankment. He had seen the chimney silhouetted against the skyline and had run breathlessly for shelter. He sat huddled close to the wall of the derelict building, for that was the place which afforded most protection from the wind and rain. The tramp took rolls of newspaper from inside his long dirty overcoat and wrapped them round himself. Then he lay on the wet earth, his coat pulled high over his neck. His face, which was overgrown with hair, slumped forward. Occasionally he sniffed loudly and from time to time he coughed. It was a deep cough, which shook his whole body, rustling the newspaper.

At seven o'clock it still wasn't light. The tramp sat up, shivering. The newspapers were soaking. The rain had penetrated through the coat. He put a hand deep into one of the pockets and took out the stub of a cigarette. It was damp and falling apart. He placed it with shaking hand in the corner of his mouth and found a match in the other pocket. He struck it time and again on the wall of the mine. Finally it spluttered into flame. By cupping his hands to his face and puffing strongly he managed to make the cigarette light.

The tramp struggled groaning to his feet. The newspapers fell from his body. He went over to the door and gazed out over the slackheaps to the black outlines of the houses beyond. He held the cigarette with his fingernails and even when there was all but nothing left of it he flicked off the glowing end and put what remained into his pocket.

Another train rushed along the line. The tramp brought his hands up to his startled face. He was like an animal caught in the glare of a car's headlights. After the train had gone he unbuttoned his overcoat. Underneath he wore only an old pair of baggy trousers tied at the waist with string. His chest was bare and covered with thick black hair, which almost hid a tattoo of a woman in a bathing-costume. On the inside of the coat there was a third pocket. From it he pulled a wrinkled paper bag. In it there were hard, warped slices of bread, the kind of bread which people feed to birds. The tramp gnawed at one of the crusts, breaking off hard pieces with his teeth. He chewed it round and round in his mouth. After eating two slices he stuffed the paper bag into his pocket again and buttoned up the overcoat. He went inside the mine and felt the newspapers with his hand. They were drenched. None of them was worth keeping. He held his back with one arm and straightened with great difficulty. Then he ambled slowly across the slackheaps towards town into the fresh September dawn.

* * *

Two hours later Max and Ben walked on the same ground. Max had woken early, relieved to find that the skies had cleared. He told Mum they were going to watch the workmen on the building-site. He wanted to go without breakfast but she wouldn't let him.

He found the torch on the back shelf of the car, and there was a length of rope in the boot. Dad had left them there in case the car ever broke down. The batteries didn't work, and slimy, white acid oozed out of the ends of them. Fortunately Max had fifteen pence in his savings tin, and he was able to buy two new batteries at the shop on the edge of the estate.

When Max got home breakfast was ready. Mum asked why he was in such a hurry if they were only going to watch the workmen. Max shrugged his shoulders. He couldn't think of an excuse. In his mind he was planning how to climb down the mine. It oughtn't to be difficult. It was the same as climbing any ladder. In fact it would be easier, because he wouldn't be able to see the ground below: and if he held the torch in his teeth both his hands would be free. There was nothing to it. It wouldn't take more than five minutes. Max drank the last of his tea and stood up. He felt a rhythm of excitement coursing through his body. He could see himself flying the aeroplane outside the house, but he could also see the overgrown black hole and no matter how hard he tried to reassure himself, the hole frightened him. He told himself it would be all right, but really he knew that what he was about to do was dangerous, and if he fell he might never come out of the mine alive. It was only an aeroplane after all. Yesterday he might have been able to forget about it. But today, now Ben had that beautiful ship, it was a matter of life and death that he should recover the aeroplane.

Mum made them put on their school raincoats in case it rained again.

'It feels cold to me, Max,' she said when he objected. She fastened Ben's top button for him as they went out of the door.

Max wanted Ben with him and yet he didn't. Ben was afraid. Max could tell that by the expression on his face. The fear conveyed itself to Max, making the black hole jump in front of his eyes. Max made himself stand straight and walk boldly. He imagined they were setting out on a dangerous expedition. That cheered him. Everybody who went on dangerous expeditions returned. He counted the paving-stones along the street, so that he was able to think of nothing.

They crossed the building-site. Ben said 'Hello' to a man who was laying bricks on a wall. Max hurried on. Then the slackheaps lay in front of them. As they came into open ground the wind suddenly hit them. It whipped at the ends of their raincoats and chapped their cheeks red. Going up the sides of the heaps, they had to push against the wind.

Ben had brought the ship with him. It was at the bottom of his coat pocket. He had made it his mascot. As long as he had the ship with him nothing could go wrong. There wasn't a hole in the pocket, but every few steps he touched the bulge where the ship was, just to be certain it was still there.

They were tired from battling with the wind when they reached the mine. They struggled for breath in the shelter of the doorway. Then with pounding heart Ben saw the newspapers.

'Where did they come from?' he gasped, pointing to the sodden grey mass on the ground.

'How do I know where they came from,' Max said angrily. 'Anyway what difference do a few newspapers make?'

'Somebody's been here,' Ben whispered in a terrified voice. 'I know they have. I can feel it.'

What a stupid brother he had, Max thought. How could he feel somebody who wasn't there?

'The newspapers must have blown here in the night,' Max told Ben impatiently. 'Somebody probably threw them out of the train.'

For a moment Ben was pacified. But then he saw the footprints leading to and from the mine. They were quite clear in the black coal-dust. They stretched as far as the eye could see.

'And what if somebody has been here? You can see for yourself they've gone away now.'

'It's the ghost. That's who it is. It's the ghost of the mine,' Ben said very seriously. Max glared at him. He wanted to laugh. So Ben had believed him the night before last. He really thought there was a ghost.

'There aren't any such things as ghosts, you big baby,' Max told him scornfully.

'I want to go home,' Ben said, his lips quivering, 'the ghost will catch us if we stay here.'

'There isn't any ghost, fathead. I was the ghost. It was only pretend.'

But Ben would not be convinced.

'Then who's been here? Whose are these footprints?'

'What does it matter whose footprints they are?'

'But nobody ever comes here. We've never seen anybody here before and those footprints aren't ours.' And to prove it Ben placed his own shoe in the nearest huge print.

'It's the ghost. I know it is. He's down the hole, and he'll be waiting for you when you climb down the ladder.'

Why had he ever brought Ben with him, Max thought. Now he too felt uncertain and frightened. He knew there was no ghost, but the blackness of the hole and the stillness of the mine unnerved him. It had been different at home in bed. Now in the daytime going down the ladder seemed impossible.

But there was something inside Max which made him go on. Perhaps if Ben had not been there he would have felt no necessity to be brave.

'You're a stupid fat idiot,' he told Ben viciously. Ben turned away deeply hurt. The words numbed him. He had to fight to prevent himself from crying.

'Hold the torch,' Max ordered. He unbuckled the belt of his coat, took it off and laid it on the ground beside the newspapers.

'All you have to do is give me the torch when I tell

you,' Max said harshly. 'Do you understand?' Ben nodded his head. He hadn't the courage or the strength to argue further.

Max led Ben out of the chimney over to the brickwork surrounding the shaft. On the inside of the bricks the earth had crumbled away to where the ladder started. Max undid the rope from his waist and tied it round a rusty nail which jutted upwards from between the bricks. He hesitated at the edge of the shaft. Now the moment had actually come he too wanted to go home. But there was no turning back. Max lifted one foot over the brickwork and tried to feel for the ladder. It wasn't there. He lifted the second foot over, all the time holding the rope tightly. He dislodged a stone. It bounced from one side of the shaft to the other and then after what seemed an age it splashed into the water below. Max's throat tightened with fear. His legs and arms were shaking. He couldn't stop them.

Slowly he lowered himself by the rope. At last he found the ladder. It was slippery. He pressed hard with his whole weight. The rung was quite solid.

'Put the torch in my mouth,' he said hoarsely to Ben. Ben stretched forward. He couldn't reach.

'Sit on the bricks. You won't fall,' Max told him. Ben obediently did what he was told.

'You haven't turned it on,' Max said impatiently. Ben scrambled back. He found the button and pushed it forward. There was a click as the light came on. He stretched out again. Max was beneath him. Only his head was above the brickwork. His open mouth was a long way away. Ben gripped the stonework with his free hand, and edged forward. He could smell the stale smell of the shaft coming up into his face. His hand couldn't quite reach. Max leaned away from the ladder, still holding on with one hand, and took the torch in his teeth.

Ben looked down. There was complete blackness. The back of his legs went wobbly. He watched Max slowly descend. The torch lit up the flesh on his face, making it like a skull. Then Ben panicked. His head was dizzy. For a moment he thought he was going to fall. He lifted his feet over the brickwork and threw himself towards the ground. He went a few inches and then something tugged violently at his chest. He tore furiously in terror. There was a loud ripping sound. His coat was caught on the nail. He ought to have remembered it before he jumped. His pulling had torn a jagged hole more than six inches long. He was caught. Ben tugged again. The coat tore a little further but it didn't come loose. With trembling hands he reached for the nail. He only just managed to touch it by twisting his whole body round inside the coat. But no matter how hard he tried he was not able to disentangle it. Then he realized why. He was lying on the ground. The nail was above him. He would have to go back on top of the brickwork. If he did that the coat would be slack and not taut.

He relaxed a few seconds, wet his lips, and drew in a deep breath. It wouldn't take long. And when he was free he would go out on to the slackheaps till Max

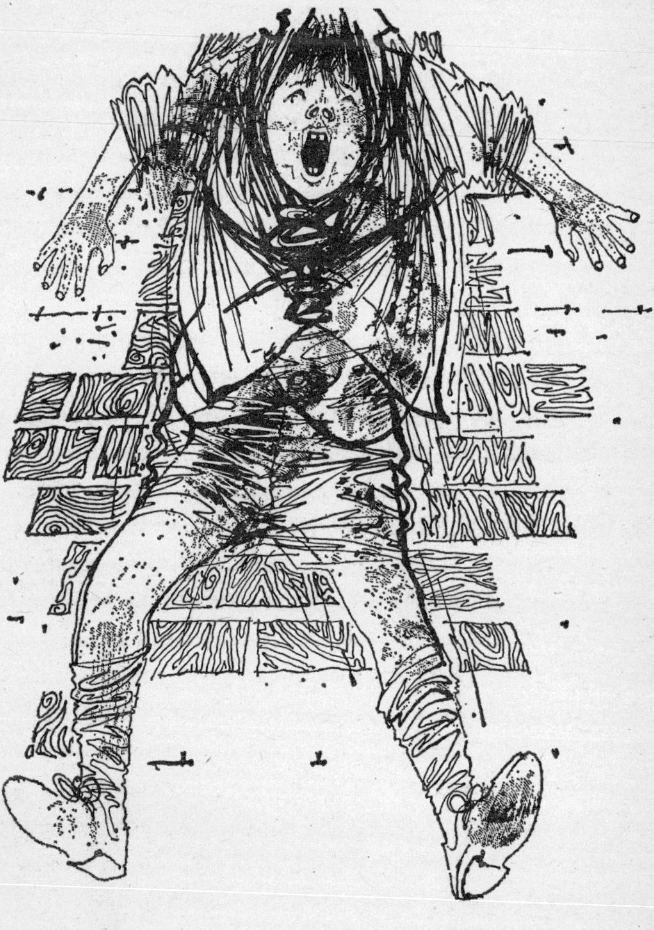

came up. He edged forward, dragging himself up the brickwork. As he moved the coat became even more entangled. This time he didn't struggle. He let his body relax. He tried to think. He could wait till Max climbed out of the shaft. That was one answer. But no. Why hadn't he thought of it before? There was a simple solution and that was to take the coat off. As the idea came to him Ben experienced a surge of pleasure and satisfaction that he had solved this difficulty on his own.

He rolled slowly and carefully to the ground. He undid the buttons one by one. So far so good, he thought. The next thing was to take his body out of the coat. He bent one arm and pulled the sleeve loose with the other hand. After that it was simple. He stood up and lifted the coat from the nail. He was so relieved, he twirled the coat above his head and made a jump to the doorway of the mine. As he did so something fell away from the raincoat pocket. At first Ben did not realize what it was. Then his eye caught the red mast. His heart lurched. It was his ship. He had forgotten all about the ship. Before he landed his feet had twisted backwards. Every nerve in his body moved towards that small wooden shape. But he was too late. The ship landed on the brickwork, toppled and then dropped into the blackness of the shaft. So quickly had it happened, Ben could not be certain his eyes had not deceived him.

He grasped the coat to his body and felt all over it with the flat of his hand. The ship was not there. His hands shot through both pockets. It was gone. He searched amongst the black coal-dust at the foot of the brickwork but there was no mistake. The ship was at the bottom of the shaft.

And now he cared whether Max climbed the ladder. Before it had only been one of Max's adventures, in which he had to take part. But now Max was doing something dangerous as much for Ben as for himself. Ben suddenly wanted to know where Max was.

He clambered up the brickwork. This time he did not think of falling.

'Max,' Ben called desperately. Max looked up. Ben could see his face clearly in the light of the torch.

'Coming,' Max answered. His voice echoed up the shaft.

'Max, I've dropped my ship. It's down there with your aeroplane.'

Max snorted through his nose. He didn't reply.

'Max, my ship,' Ben shouted again. He screwed his eyes together to try and see more clearly in the darkness. The torch was coming upwards slowly. Max couldn't have found it. Ben groaned, almost in tears.

He could hear Max panting and grunting as he came nearer. First his head appeared, then his whole body. His face and hair were covered in black slime. It was on his jacket and trousers as well. Max pulled himself up the rope and jumped clear of the brickwork. He spat the torch from his mouth and stood, his back bent, his hands resting on his knees.

Max hadn't found the ship. Ben knew he hadn't.

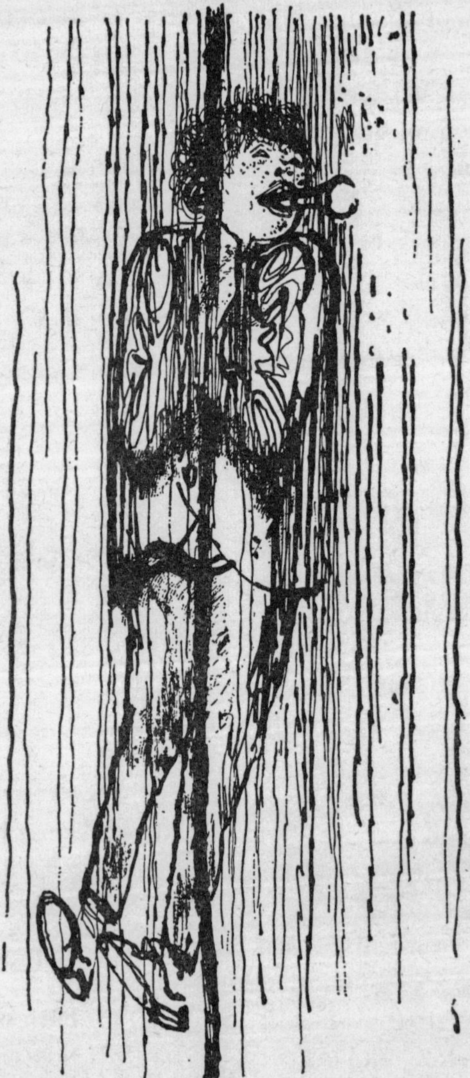

There was no bulge under his jumper or in his pockets.

'It was too far,' Max gasped, 'I went part of the way but it was too far to the bottom.' Ben bit his lip. What he dreaded was true. The ship was lost. The one valuable thing he had ever owned was gone. What would he tell Mr Mansion? When he thought of the policeman he instinctively looked towards the houses. His eyes were only half-focused. His mind was still on the ship. But he saw the figure walking across the slackheaps towards them. The realization of what was before his eyes made him wake up. 'Max,' he whispered, grasping his brother by the arm, 'over there. Look!' Max straightened and brushed the hair from his face. He hadn't been listening to Ben's words but in an instant he too had seen the figure. He pushed Ben behind the brickwork out of view.

It was a man, though he was too far away yet to make out what he looked like. He was coming in the direction of the mine.

What did he want? What could anybody want at the mine? Was it possible that he already knew they were there? Whoever it was he mustn't find them. They had to escape.

There was one chance. The slackheaps dipped down into a valley before they rose to the mine. When the man was at the bottom of the valley they would be hidden, and if they went round the back of the heap he wouldn't be able to see them.

Max tugged the sleeve of Ben's jumper.

'Fetch the macks,' he said softly. Ben scrambled

almost on his stomach to the edge of the brickwork and from there to the mine. His foot dislodged a loose stone. It went rolling down the side of the heap. Max waved his hands frantically. Ben understood. He threw himself flat. Max raised his head a few inches. The man was still walking. He hadn't heard.

Max beckoned to Ben with a jerk of his head. Ben cautiously scrambled to his brother's side.

'Remember, stay close to me and run when I tell you,' Max hissed. It would be just like Ben to get them both caught, he thought. And it very nearly happened. As the man reached the valley and began the last climb to the mine, he disappeared out of sight. Max began to run, dragging Ben with him. They had only gone a few yards when Ben's shoe came off. He slithered in the wet coal-dust and fell. Max ran back for it, took Ben by the hand, and hauled him to his feet. There was no time to lose. The man would be able to see them in a few seconds. Max skirted the side of the slackheap, his head held low. Ben tottered after him, half running, half skipping on one foot. They dashed down the heap. Only when they reached the bottom did Max stop and let him put his shoe on. Ben's stocking was black and his big toe stuck out through the end of it.

'Did he see us?' Ben asked, wide-eyed.

'If he didn't it wasn't your fault,' Max retorted. 'Come on! There isn't time for a rest. We'll have enough trouble without being late for dinner.'

Ben got to his feet and followed breathlessly after Max in the direction of the houses. It must have been twelve o'clock because when they reached the building-site the dumper and the cement-mixer stood unnaturally still. Ben saw a row of men's legs through the open hut door.

They stopped at a huge puddle feathered by the wind. They splashed water over their shoes, taking off the worst of the mud and coaldust.

'You go first,' Max said. 'If Mum sees my clothes we won't be allowed out for the rest of the holidays.' Ben looked at himself and then at Max. Max was right. He was like a coalman.

'If the coast is clear sit in the front window,' Max told him.

Ben left Max standing in the road and began to walk towards their house. He knew there might be a row but after the loss of the ship and the man at the mine there was nothing left to be frightened of. And luck was with them. On the kitchen table Mum had scrawled a note,

'Gone to the shops. If you're hungry there's milk in the refrigerator and biscuits in the tin.'

Ben rushed into the road and waved wildly to Max. Then he hid his coat under the front seat of the car. He would tell Mum about it when she was in a good mood.

In ten minutes they managed to clean most of the dirt from themselves. Max scrubbed his jacket and trousers with the old sponge which was kept for cleaning the bath. He was soaking, but by lying on the carpet close to the fire in the front room he somehow made himself look almost normal by the time Mum arrived home.

'And what have you two been up to?' she asked suspiciously. Ben tried not to appear guilty.

After dinner there was nothing to do. Ben wanted to go to Mr Mansion's house but he hadn't the courage. Instead they stayed in their room and read comics. Really Ben longed to return to the mine, but as Max said nothing he kept his thoughts to himself. Ben knew Max was afraid. As far as he was concerned the aeroplane and the ship were gone for ever. Ben was afraid too. He was afraid of the ladder and of the man they had seen.

As he lay on the bed, looking at the comic but not reading it, the notion came into Ben's head that he would climb down the shaft. Max hadn't been able to do it, but the aeroplane wasn't as important to Max as the ship was to Ben. He would have to try. Living without the ship seemed inconceivable to him. The question was, when would it be possible? Max rarely went anywhere on his own, and Max, Ben was positive, would not allow him to attempt an adventure that he himself had not been able to complete.

It might be a week before any such opportunity arose. Probably it would not be before they started school. Or so Ben was thinking. He was thumbing through the comic, racking his brains for a way to get rid of Max, when Mum opened their bedroom door.

'I'm going to the library. Do you want to come?' she asked.

'Oh, all right, if you like,' Max answered grumpily.

'Don't if it's too much trouble for you,' Mum said tartly.

Max stood up lazily and threw his comic on the bed.

'And how about you, Ben?' Ben hesitated. Here was his chance. But it was so unexpected. He was at a loss for words.

'Well, are you or aren't you? Make up your mind. I haven't all day to waste.' She spoke harshly. Max had put her in a bad temper.

'I'll stay and read my comic,' he finally managed to say.

'Just as you like,' Mum said. 'You collect the books together, Max, and then we'll be off.'

Soon they were ready with their coats on.

'Now don't you go bothering Mr Mansion while we're away,' Mum told Ben.

'I won't,' Ben promised truthfully.

'And there's some biscuits on the table for you,' Mum said.

'Thank you,' Ben answered.

'Goodbye.'

'Bye,' he called after them. The kitchen door banged. He was on his own. There was no time to lose. They wouldn't be away for more than an hour even if they had to wait for a bus in town. But it ought to be long enough. It wouldn't take him more than ten minutes to the mine, ten minutes back again and another ten minutes to climb up and down the ladder. Ben smiled to himself. He wondered what Max would say when he gave him his aeroplane.

The torch was underneath Max's pillow. Ben had seen him put it there at dinner time. Max had forgotten to switch it off but the light was still bright.

'I mustn't get dirty,' Ben muttered to himself. He found his old football jersey. It wouldn't matter if that was messed up.

He hesitated at the back door. Had he forgotten anything? He glanced round the kitchen. There was a plateful of chocolate biscuits on the table. He picked up two in each hand and then walked out into the street. As he went towards the building-site Ben's head was unusually clear.

He had one thought in his mind and that was the ship at the bottom of the mineshaft.

CHAPTER FIVE

Down the Rope

THE WIND had dropped. For once the slackheaps and the mine had an atmosphere of peace. The sun came through a break in the clouds, an autumnal sun with little warmth in it. The air was crisp and fresh from the previous night. The rain, which that morning had lain like a thin transparent carpet on the slackheaps, was now almost gone. Only here and there were there patches of blackened wetness. It was three o'clock, that part of the day when no trains ran past the mine. It would be another hour before the people from town began returning home again.

Ben hurried across the slackheaps. Sometimes going down he broke into a run but the upward slope forced him to walk. He had not been alone on the heaps before. Until today he would sooner have gone anywhere else.

Once he imagined Mum and Max riding on the upper deck of a yellow bus. He even glanced behind him and thought of going back. But the ship made him go on towards the red chimney which lay ahead of him. As he came nearer the mine, he searched in every direction for any sign of the man. Yet somehow he knew there was no-one there. Never before had he felt so utterly alone. He felt like a dwarf beside the huge brick chimney which towered above him. Fear gripped at his chest as he climbed the final slackheap. What would he do if the man was there? Perhaps he was hiding behind the door waiting for him. There would be no escape here, nowhere to run to.

Now he had reached level ground. The doorway was in front of him. He could see through to the dark light beyond. He waited, expecting something to happen. When nothing did, he picked up a loose lump of coal and threw it through the opening. It landed with a dull thud and then rolled with a scraping sound out of sight. The absolute silence returned, defying Ben to make the next move.

'Is anybody there?' Ben called. He had meant to shout but the words came out of his mouth as a whisper. Nobody would have heard that.

He tried again.

'Hello! Are you there?' Still there was no answer. If only Max was here, Ben thought. Max would know what to do. But Max wasn't here. He was in the library. Being without Max was like having only one hand.

Ben advanced two steps, kicking stones in front of him so as to make as much noise as possible. He came to the doorway. If the man was in there he would be able to hear his heart beating. Ben steeled himself. He held the torch above his head ready to strike. He took a quick peep and then jumped away. He had only seen for a fraction of a second but his eyes had taken in everything. The mine was empty. There was nobody here but himself. The beating of his heart returned to normal. He walked round the stack searching the empty heaps. It reminded him of looking under his bed before he turned the light off. He knew there was nothing yet he was still afraid.

When he had circled the stack twice it occurred to Ben that he was wasting time. He switched on the torch and climbed over the low brickwork to the shaft. Everything was the same as it had been that morning. The rope was tied to the rusty nail. Ben noticed a shred of his raincoat hanging from it. He lifted it off and put it in his pocket. Mum might need it when she came to mend the coat. If he had the missing patch she might be less annoyed with him.

Ben took a deep breath. Here I go, he thought. He put the torch between his teeth and edged closer to the shaft, all the time holding on to the rope in case he fell. The hole loomed up at him, black and sinister. Now he had to slide down the rope till his feet touched the topmost rung. It was the same as jumping from a wall. If you looked down or thought about it, then your nerves failed. This is what happened to Ben. The black hole drew his eyes, and no matter how hard he tried he had to look down again.

'Come on, Ben,' he whispered to himself, 'look straight ahead of you.' That was what the teacher at school said when anybody was frightened to jump from the diving-board.

Ben forced his head to stay still. He grasped the rope with both hands and swung his feet clear. His shoes scraped against the loose soil at the head of the shaft. Showers of dirt cascaded below him. Ben closed his eyes and clung on. His face itched terribly. He wanted to scratch his nose but he dared not let go. His trousers had slipped when he jumped. They felt as though they were going to fall down at any moment.

Ben opened his eyes. He was level with the brick-work. His face almost touched it. The rough, sharp patterns on the bricks and the crumbling grey cement in between was all he could see. He desperately wanted to look down to know where the ladder was. He didn't though. Once he looked down he knew he would feel dizzy.

Slowly he let the rope slip through one hand, keeping a tight grip with the other hand. His body lowered a few inches. The hard wall of the shaft rubbed against his knees. It was cold and slimy. There was a stabbing pain in his leg. He could feel warm blood trickling into his sock. The torch jarred against the wall. The handle pressed against the back of his throat. It caught the soft spot which made him want to be sick when it was touched with a finger. Ben retched. His mouth opened wide. The torch fell. Instinctively his hand went to catch it. He almost lost his balance, and only just in time did he take hold again with both hands. The torch hit his chest. Ben threw himself against it, forcing it against the shaft wall. It lodged there between his stomach and the bricks. He could feel its round outline on his body. To save it he had to let go with one hand. It was unnerving, groping when he could not see. But he found it at last and placed it back in his mouth. Dust had stuck to it, which clogged his throat.

Now his arms were aching. They seemed to be tearing themselves out by the sockets. At school he had climbed ropes. He had been able to hang on longer than anybody else in his class. At school, though, there was the mat underneath if he fell. If only he could have rested, as he could against the wall bars in the gym.

Then he panicked. He let the rope slip quickly through his hands. It tore at his skin. His feet kicked wildly, sending him from one side of the shaft to the other. He remembered to keep his mouth away from the wall. In terror he realized he was near the end of the rope, for he had been falling for some time. He closed his hands together as hard as they would go. The rope burnt like red-hot metal. He swung against the side of the shaft. His legs struck stone. His body twisted until he was almost upside down. Somehow he managed to grip the rope and prevent his mouth from hitting anything.

When he straightened out he saw his left foot was caught between two rungs of the ladder.

He had experienced a dull pain as he fell; now his leg was numb, yet underground it seemed to hurt much less. Slowly he moved his hands from the rope to the rungs. They were cold and narrow after holding the rope.

Ben took stock of the situation. He had fallen quite a long way. The round patch of daylight was far above his head. And he had been right. He had stopped just in time. By shining the torch downwards he could see the black binding which was wound round the last few inches of the rope. It was a miracle that the torch hadn't fallen out of his mouth. But the miracle had happened. He had to go on. How much time had passed since he left the house he could not guess. It seemed a lifetime away.

His arms were aching even worse. He lowered one foot and felt for the next rung. It pressed upwards through his shoe to the sole of his foot. His body was stretched out tight against the ladder. He let go with one hand and found a more comfortable position. He had moved down one rung. His breath came quickly. I'll never do it, Ben thought. He took the torch out of his mouth and shone it around him. The end of the rope swayed like a pendulum beside his head. It seemed to invite him to take hold of it. But the thought of pulling himself up was even more difficult than go-

ing down. Either way at that moment appeared impossible. Ben rested his head against the cold rungs and let out a sob.

'What shall I do, Max?' he gasped. But there was no Max to answer. The fear of falling had come back. The water would be cold. And he couldn't swim. Nobody would hear him shouting. What would happen to him? Why hadn't he told Max? Max could have saved him.

The stabbing numbness grew worse. Ben didn't decide to go downwards. His arms and legs just went that way. After a time he got into a rhythm. It was easier now. He was tired all right but it was as though there was a slowly unwinding spring inside him, which moved his hands and feet half against his will.

Most of the time he kept his eyes closed. There was nothing to see if he opened them except for the rungs of the ladder. Down and down he went. It was easier to go on than stop. So on he went. Once he rested, Ben knew, he might be too tired to start again.

Twice when he felt for the next rung with his foot there was nothing. The rung had probably rusted and fallen away. Fortunately the one beneath it was there and it stood under his weight.

He knew he ought to think how he would climb back but for the present he pushed the thought from his mind. All that mattered was that he was going downward, further and further and further.

He reached the bottom sooner than he had expected. Gradually the air changed. It became moist and dank-smelling, like the smell that rises from a stagnant pool.

By the side of the ladder a stone jutted out from the shaft. It was no larger than a small cushion. Ben clutched on to it. Since he had jumped on to the rope this was the first opportunity he had had to rest. With relief he took the torch from his mouth. He spat out what remained of the dirt and shone the light downwards. It was a bright light, brighter than he had ever imagined a torch light could be. The beam splayed outwards, finishing in a number of ripples, rather like the ripples in a pond when it is raining. The ripples caught different colours, dark greens, browns and blues. For a moment Ben could not distinguish the forms. Then his eyes focused and he saw a most remarkable sight.

The shaft finished a few feet below the stone shelf he was sitting on, at least water came to that level. It was black, filthy water. Ben could smell it. The surface of the water was broken in many places by debris which protruded upwards. In the middle was a blue pram, twisted and rusted almost beyond recognition. And around it were clothes, disintegrating newspaper, a chair with its back torn off, a bottomless bucket, an enormous vase and the wringer from a washing-machine.

Ben's eyes picked them out one by one. Suddenly his heart gave a jump. He scrambled off the ledge on to the ladder. He had seen the red mast of the ship. It was sticking out from the side of the pram. He was so excited he did not bother to put the torch in his mouth. He managed with one hand, running down the rungs as if they were stairs. The possibility of recovering the ship made him forget the misery of the climb.

As he came nearer the smell caught in his nostrils. It had been there on the ladder but now it was much stronger, a nauseating, sickly smell. Ben held his breath. He placed the torch in his mouth, knelt on the last rung of the ladder and reached out. The pram was too far away, but by standing up and stretching with his foot he managed to drag it towards him. He caught hold of the bar and pulled the heavy weight through the water. Objects bobbed to the surface around him. Ben took no notice of them. His eyes were on the pram. His hand clutched at the ship, which had lodged between the spokes of a wheel. And then he had it. Feeling the smooth surface of the wood brought back the memory of Mr Mansion's kind face and the small, warm hut.

Ben slipped the ship under his jumper. He was about to climb the ladder when the beam of the torch caught a skeleton half-submerged in the water. The sight of it made him shudder. He could not bear anything dead. It was about the size of a cat, but it was impossible to say what it had been, for only the bones remained. Beside the skeleton was Max's aeroplane.

Ben hesitated. Now he had the ship he ought to take the aeroplane too. But the skeleton shocked him. Its white bones grimed over with slime shone in the light of the torch. He turned his head to the ladder. He couldn't bear to look. With his foot he felt in the water where he thought the aeroplane had been. His shoe struck something. He dragged it towards him and trapped it against the wall of the shaft. When he shone the torch down he saw with relief that it was the aeroplane. But then as he groped for it with his free hand his feet slipped on the wet rung. Too late he fought for his balance. He couldn't prevent himself from falling. His body banged against the pram. He sank up to his chest. The touch of the water made him fight. He grasped the nearest rung and pulled himself upwards. Water poured from his shoes, socks and trousers. It wasn't cold water but the fear of falling made him shiver all over.

He crouched on the bottom rung gasping for breath. The smell was terrible now. It came not only from the water, it was on him as well. One thing at least: he hadn't lost the torch. He shone it down. The skeleton had disappeared. At least he could not see it. But Max's aeroplane was there. It was right next to the bottom rung. All he had to do was pick it up. He shook off the loose water and stuffed it in the top of his jersey beside the ship.

A sudden joy surged through his heart. He had done it. Where Max had attempted and failed, he had succeeded. Already he could see himself running homewards across the slackheaps. What Mum might say was of no significance compared with the admiration Max would have for him.

He hitched up his trousers. He was ready to start back. As he began to climb the smell returned. It caught in his throat and made him cough. When he reached the shelf he was exhausted. He sat down on the hard stone and rested his body against the wall of the shaft.

He put his hand inside his jumper and took out the ship. It was then he noticed that the light was not as bright as it had been. He shook the torch. The light stayed the same. The battery was becoming weaker. Soon he would have nothing to see by. How many rungs were there above him? He couldn't remember.

He slid the ship back inside his jumper and stood up. He put the torch in his mouth and started climbing. One rung, two rungs, three rungs, four rungs. When he got to the fifth one he had to stop. He was gasping for breath. There didn't seem to be enough air. It made him cough again. Though his clothes were wet he felt hot. Sweat ran down his forehead into his eyes. But he forced himself to go on. He pulled himself up to the sixth rung. The heat was even greater. It was stifling him. He had to rest.

The beam from the torch was dimmer. The light was no longer white now but a dull orange-brown colour. Ben made a desperate effort. With all his strength he tried to lift himself to the next rung. His body heaved and then sank back. He couldn't do it. He would have to wait. Going upwards was much more difficult than coming down. Slowly he lowered himself to the stone. He sank on to it with relief. The air and the smell were making him ill. If only he could have escaped from them, then he might have been able to think.

The light was almost gone. It flickered on and off, barely illuminating the opposite wall of the shaft. A minute later he was in darkness. It was a terrifying thick blackness he had never experienced before. A red line stayed for a few moments where the wire in the bulb was. Then that too went. Any courage Ben had previously possessed ebbed from him.

With the blackness came a silence. It was a stillness like death. There was no living being here except himself. Ben began to cry, tears of loneliness and fear. Nobody knew where he was. They would never find him. He would die in the mine. His body would fall in the water and all that would be left would be his skeleton, like the skeleton of that animal. His sobs echoed in the narrow shaft, making him even more afraid and lonely.

He cried and cried until he could cry no more. He was so tired. If only he had been able to stretch out his cramped body. Any thought he had of climbing the ladder was now gone. His head lolled on to his shoulder. Once he almost fell. Whether it was night or day he had no idea.

Later, much later, there was a splash beneath him. He sat upright with a start. Had he been dreaming? No, there it was again. It was like the sound of an animal swimming through water. Ben held his breath. What could it be? There was something down there in the water. He pressed his body flat against the wall. It was the ghost of the mine. The ghost had come to get him. It must be the ghost. What else could it be?

Ben reached for the rung above his head. He tried to lever himself up but he couldn't do it. The lower part of his body had gone dead. He sank on to the shelf and closed his eyes. He was in a stupor. His mouth opened wide and he gasped as a fish does when it is taken out of water.

What did the ghost look like? What would it do to him? Ben imagined it grasping him with its slimy hands and pulling him down, down, down into the water.

CHAPTER SIX

Lost

MAX AND Mum had to wait nearly a quarter of an hour for the bus to the library. It was the middle of the afternoon. The library was quiet. There were only six people there beside themselves. The librarians ambled leisurely from shelf to shelf placing the books back from the trolleys. There was nobody at the desk to give them their tickets for the books they had returned so Mum told Max to go and choose the books he wanted. She went to the mystery and romance shelf. She always read that sort of book.

Max sat on the old brown chair in the corner of the children's section. The air was clammy and the light from the round electric shades hurt Max's eyes. He had a headache. He didn't really want a book. The only thing he could think about was getting home to see the play on television at five o'clock. He knew it was a good one because he had seen it described in the *Radio Times*.

Ten minutes later he was still sitting glumly on the chair, his hands deep in his pockets. Mum walked over to him. Onc of her books had a picture on the front of it of a man lying in a coffin with a knife in his stomach.

'Haven't you found what you want yet?' she asked, a note of impatience in her voice. 'Hurry up, I've some shopping to do and we're late already.' Max picked up the first book he could find and slithered off the chair.

It took the woman at the desk ages to find the tickets and stamp their books. Max was bored. He wished he had stayed at home with Ben.

He dawdled after Mum through the swinging doors. She let them go. They swung to and nearly hit Max in the face. Mum told him to pick his feet up. After that Max didn't do a single thing she asked him. He dropped the string-bag she gave him to carry and in the supermarket he took a packet of bubblegum without her permission. Max knew she was annoyed. He ought to have known better than to provoke her further. But then Max was annoyed himself.

When they came to the cash desk he sat down on a large cardboard box and blew huge pink bubbles through his teeth. 'Don't, Max,' Mum told him when she saw what he was doing. Max heaved a great sigh. He stretched the gum out of his mouth in a long string.

'You filthy child,' she said loudly. Everybody in the shop turned and stared at Max. He stuffed the gum back in his mouth and stood up.

'Hold these,' Mum ordered, pushing the string-bag full of tins into his hands. Max was worn out. Having to carry this weight was the last straw. He staggered after Mum muttering to himself. One of the shopgirls with a shiny blue coat held the door open for them.

When they got outside Mum turned on him, her face red with anger.

'If you behave like a savage in a shop again I'll knock your block off,' she shouted, 'and I don't care if it is in front of other people. Disgracing me like that!' Max drew in a deep breath and stared at the pavement. What an afternoon it had been. Why hadn't he stayed with Ben?

It was almost the rush hour. The streets were overflowing with people. Streams of cars edged along the road, coming to a standstill every time the traffic lights changed to red. The bus queue was three shops long. It stretched in an untidy line like the tail of a prehistoric monster. Max dropped the string-bag on the pavement at the end of the queue. Mum didn't say a word to him.

They had to wait ages for a bus and when they finally did reach home it was a quarter to six. Max sank into Mum's armchair. The television play had finished five minutes ago. Mum came through from the kitchen.

'Where's Ben?' she asked. Max shook his head.

'I don't know,' he said. 'Must be somewhere I suppose.'

'Have a look for him, Max. Tell him tea's nearly ready.'

'Where shall I look?' Max asked grumpily. He was still sulking from the row in the supermarket.

'Go and see if he's with Mr Mansion, there's a good boy,' Mum said coaxingly.

Max sighed. With great effort he pulled himself to his feet and walked into the kitchen.

'What's for tea?' he asked, sniffing to see if he could smell it.

'If you're quick and find Ben I'll make your favourite.'

'What's that?' Max asked, as if he didn't know.

'Eggs, bacon, tomatoes and beans.'

'And chips!' Max said.

'All right and chips,' Mum agreed.

That cheered Max up. At least they were having a good tea. He went from the warm kitchen to the chill, evening air outside. There weren't any lights on in Mr Mansion's house. Max rapped on the glass of the front door. There was no sound or movement from inside. Max waited and knocked again. Still there was no answer. Perhaps they're in the shed, Max thought. But there wasn't a light there either, and when Max tried the handle he found it was locked.

'He isn't at Mr Mansion's house,' Max told Mum.

'Don't be silly, Max, he must be there.'

'I tell you he isn't. I knocked three times and there was no answer.'

'He's probably in the shed. I bet you didn't look there.'

'Yes I did,' Max retorted.

'You eat your tea and I'll go and see for myself.'

Mum dished out the eggs, bacon, tomatoes, beans and chips on to two plates. She put one of them out for Max. Then she lit the oven and put Ben's plate inside. Max hardly noticed her as she went out of the door.

He sat at the table, his plate piled high in front of him. He took salt between his fingertips and sprinkled it over the chips. He was just about to begin when he remembered the red sauce. Mum had forgotten to put it out for him. He reached over to the wall cupboard for it and trailed the bottle upside down round the outside of his plate. If Mum had been there she wouldn't have allowed him to take nearly so much. He attacked the food with the fork. It tasted so good he couldn't eat it quickly enough. Red sauce dribbled over his chin. He wiped it off with the back of his hand and sucked it into his mouth.

Mum still hadn't come back. She was being a long time. Max held up his plate and licked it clean, his tongue flicking in and out like a lizard's. He was just about to steal a few of Ben's chips when he heard footsteps on the gravel path. He quickly sat on his stool and placed the knife and fork neatly towards him on the plate.

Mum came in looking worried. She had been hurrying. Her face was flushed. Max could tell she was upset.

'He isn't there,' she said, 'and the people next door say Mr Mansion is working late today.'

'He might be on the building-site,' Max suggested. 'I'll go and see if you like.'

'Oh, will you, Max? That is good of you. It's cold outside. You'd better put your coat on.' She helped him on with it and fastened the buttons; a thing she only did with Max when she wanted him to hurry.

'He is a naughty boy. Making us worry like this. He knows when tea is. People would think he hadn't a home to go to.' She spoke more to herself than to Max.

'Try not to be long,' she called after him as he ran down the street. At the corner Max turned and looked back. She was still standing there, her huge figure outlined in the light cast by the open kitchen door. 'Stupid little brother,' Max muttered to himself. 'I'll eat his tea if he doesn't come soon.'

The building-site was deserted. There was only the night watchman warming his hands over a blazing brazier. Max walked quietly towards him. He had never spoken to the man before and he was a little afraid of him. He stopped between the planks, the pile of bricks and the freshly-dug earth. His foot caught a loose stone. The man gave a start and then he saw Max.

'Here! What do you want?' he exclaimed.

'It's my little brother,' Max said. 'I've lost my little brother.'

'I ain't seen no-one,' the man replied sullenly. He turned back to the fire, poking it with a long stick.

'He's called Ben,' Max went on. 'He's not as tall as I am and he's got big ears.' The man didn't answer. Perhaps he's deaf, Max thought.

'He's not come home and my mum's worried about him,' Max shouted.

'Ain't been no-one here since I came on,' the man said. He sniffed loudly and then began raking the fire again.

Max stood waiting, expecting the man to say more, but he didn't. Max turned and picked his way between the planks to the road. There was thick mud sticking to the underside of his shoes, making them heavy and difficult to walk in. As Max kicked it off on the side of the pavement, he looked up and his eye caught the dull black outlines of the slackheaps against the night sky.

'He couldn't have gone there,' Max said to himself. 'He wouldn't have gone there on his own.' But as he walked back up the street Max was filled with a certainty that the only place where Ben could be was the mine.

Mum was standing outside the kitchen door talking across the fence to Mr and Mrs Johns.

'Saw him after you left,' Mrs Johns was saying, 'wearing a football jersey he was. Shot out of your house as if the devil was after him, I says at the time. Didn't I, Jim?'

'That you did, Edna,' Mr Johns agreed, puffing at his pipe.

'I says to Jim, What in the world's the matter with the boy, dressing himself up in that outfit? Well, then he went tearing off down the street and we didn't see him after that.'

'He isn't there,' Max said, when Mrs Johns paused for breath.

'Well, did you have a proper look?' Mum asked him.

'I saw the night watchman and I searched on my own as well.'

'Oh, dearie me. What are we going to do now?' Max knew she was almost in tears. He wished she wouldn't cry.

Then Mrs Johns remembered she had a cake in the oven. She rushed into her kitchen saying, 'I do hope it's not spoilt.'

'Let us know if there's anything we can do,' Mr Johns said, going in after her.

'Are you sure he wasn't there?' Mum asked Max.

'I did look, honest I did, Mum,' Max said. 'If he had been there I'd have found him.' Mum raised her hand to her face and wiped the tears from her eyes.

'He could have gone to the library after us. And then when we were shopping he might have missed us.' Max really didn't believe it. He only told Mum that in an effort to cheer her up.

'Let's go inside and have a cup of tea,' Mum said. 'We'll wait ten minutes, and if he isn't home then we'll have to call the police.'

Mum boiled the kettle and added water to the teapot. As they went in the front room she glanced into the oven.

'His tea will be shrivelled up,' she complained. Max nearly asked if he could eat it but then he decided he had better not.

They sat in the armchairs by the window. Each time there were footsteps outside Mum stood up and hurried to the door. But every time it was somebody coming home from work, who lived further up the street. The minutes ticked by on the mantelpiece clock. Five minutes past seven, six minutes past, seven minutes past.

Suddenly Max felt frightened. Mum would blame it

on him. Ben must have gone right to the mine and he was climbing down the ladder. That was the only explanation there could be.

'I want you to think,' Mum was saying, 'I want you to think where Ben could have gone to.' Max hesitated. Should he tell her the truth?

'I don't know, Mum,' he found himself answering, 'I just can't think where he could be.'

'He wouldn't have gone further than the building-site?' she asked anxiously.

Max tried to look her in the eye without flinching.

'He wouldn't go there, Mum,' he said, trying to put conviction into his voice.

While he was speaking he thought how he could know for sure whether Ben had gone down the ladder. If the torch was still under his pillow he couldn't have gone, for without the torch he would not be able to see.

More time slipped by. It was almost half-past seven now. The street was empty and quiet. Everybody had returned home from work. The light was changing. It would not be long before it was dark.

'I'm waiting one more minute,' Mum finally said. Max watched the minute hand on the clock. For an age it seemed to stick just before the thirty mark. Suddenly it hovered, then it moved the last minute, too quick for the eye to follow.

Mum got to her feet. She picked her coat up from the sofa and tied a scarf round her head. She took one last look out of the window and then turned to Max.

'If Ben comes home before I get back you're both to

wait here for me. Do you understand?' Max nodded his head.

'I understand, Mum,' he said.

Then she was gone. She forgot to close the kitchen door behind her, a thing she was for ever reminding Max and Ben about. Max opened one of the side windows and leaned out. Already she had disappeared round the corner of the street.

Max dashed into his bedroom. The torch was not where he had left it. He crawled right underneath the bed in case it had rolled but it was not there. Max knew he had to do something. But if Ben was stuck at the bottom of the mine he wouldn't be able to bring him up on his own. Why hadn't he told Mum? He couldn't save Ben by himself. A dull threatening feeling weighed down inside him. It was all too much for him. He stood in the middle of the living-room floor, torn between running to the mine and staying where he was.

He went out into the road. The cold air blew through his jumper. There wasn't a soul in sight.

'I've got to go,' he said to himself. As he made the decision Mum's words came back to him. 'If Ben comes home you're both to wait.' But she hadn't said what he was to do if Ben didn't return. In any case Ben was probably in danger. There was no use thinking about it. Something had to be done.

Max reached the building-site before he realized he wouldn't be able to see once he left the houses behind. He tore back to the house. The kitchen door was still open. He had remembered Dad's oil lamp. Dad bought it two years ago when they were on holiday in Wales. It was the sort miners had used in the olden days. Dad had seen it in an antique shop and they had all gone into the shop together and bought it. When they came home he had put it on the mantelpiece and in the evenings he had lit it for Max and Ben as a special treat before they went to bed. But after a few weeks the metal changed colour and Mum said she wasn't having it in the front room. So she had stored it away in Dad's wardrobe.

There was a key to the wardrobe and it was still in the lock. Max turned it and pulled open the door. The lamp was there standing behind a row of shirts. Max picked it up with shaking hands and shook it. He could hear the oil splashing around inside. There wasn't very much. But it would be sufficient.

Max snatched a box of matches from the gas stove. Then he raced back down the street holding the lamp by its wire handle. It swung to and fro, the clouded glass rattling. Dad had never allowed them to light the lamp but Max knew how it was done. The small wheel at the side was turned until the wick appeared. It was ready to light with a match then. That was all there was to it.

Max tore round the outside of the building-site. The slackheaps loomed ahead, towering mountains of blackness, hardly distinguishable from the night sky. Max ran so fast that before he knew it he had reached the mine. He made himself slow down, breathing deeply to regain his wind.

When he looked up the stranger they had seen that morning was standing in the doorway of the chimney. He was leaning against the wall, his hands in his overcoat pockets. He stared at Max for several moments in the same way an animal does when it is caught unawares.

'Please, mister,' Max said, advancing the last few yards. The man backed into the shadows. Max followed him. He felt no fear. Instead the man had suddenly given him hope. Here was somebody who could help. The thought that there might be any sort of danger never crossed Max's mind.

Max stopped at the doorway. The man had sat down on the newspapers. He had taken a crust of bread out of one of his pockets and he was gnawing at it.

'Get away from here, you,' he said harshly when he saw Max. He spoke as if the mine belonged to him, as if it was his home.

'I've lost my little brother,' Max said desperately, 'and I think he's climbed the ladder into the mine.' The man stopped gnawing and examined Max closely. Max knew he didn't believe him.

'He dropped his ship down there this morning,' Max tried to explain, 'and he's gone to fetch it. Only he must be stuck, and now he can't get out.'

The man stood up and came towards Max. He climbed over the low wall of the doorway. Max didn't know what he was going to do. He stayed perfectly still, a little afraid now that the man was so close to him. The man went on chewing and there was a strange expression on his face as though he could not make up his mind.

'You pulling my leg?' he finally said.

'No, honest I'm not. It's the truth. I swear it is,' Max answered. He drew a cross on his chest with his finger. There was a long silence.

'What you got there?' the man said, pointing at the lamp. Max eagerly held it for him to see.

'There's oil in it and it will light,' Max told him. The man grunted. He took hold of the lamp and unscrewed the cap where the oil was poured. He brought the hole close to his nose and sniffed. He nodded, screwed the cap on again, and then walked over to the shaft. With a jerk of the head he beckoned Max to follow.

'You call to him,' he said. 'See if he can hear you.'

Max moved alongside the wall. The rope was still there loosely hanging down the opening. He cupped his hands to his mouth and shouted,

'Ben! Can you hear me? Are you there, Ben?' He waited, straining his ears, but there was no sound. Max turned to the man to see if he should try again, but the man gave him no response. He was busy screwing up the wheel. When he had done it he laid the lamp on the ground. From one of his pockets he took a match and struck it against the rough brickwork. He protected the flame from the wind with his other hand. As the wick caught fire it lit up the side of his face. His skin was rough and dirty and his hair came down over the top of his coat.

The man held the lamp above the black hole of the

shaft. He leaned far out over the brickwork, so far that Max thought he was going to fall. Then he shouted,

'Are you down there, laddie? Answer me if you can hear.' His coarse loud voice filled the whole landscape. It echoed down the shaft, bounced back again and then died on the still night air. The man shouted once, twice, three times, but there was no reply from the bottom of the mine.

CHAPTER SEVEN

Ghosts in the Mine

BEN SAT upright on the shelf. Without meaning to he had fallen asleep. How he had done so on that hard stone and with wet clothes on he could not understand. Something had woken him. Then he remembered the ghost. He sat perfectly still, afraid he would hear something. Yes, there was a noise. It was coming from above. He was sure he had heard it in the back of his mind when he had been asleep. Now, there it was again. It was very distant, but Ben was certain it was a voice. The voice of the ghost, he thought. The ghost was after him. His time had come.

Ben was fully awake. He felt behind him on the stone. One of the bricks was loose. He clawed at it with his fingernails. Very slowly it moved. And then the voice came again. He pulled frantically with a strength he had not known he possessed. The brick grated and slid away from the wall. It was so heavy he almost dropped it. He reached behind him again, and loosened two more bricks. They came loose much more easily than the first one had done. He laid them beside him on the shelf, one on top of the other.

He was just in time. There was a different noise now and it was coming towards him. It must be the ghost. Who else could it be? Ben could hear the scraping of his boots on the ladder. He stood up with one of the bricks in his free hand. With the other hand he supported himself against the ladder. His legs were weak. They were hardly strong enough to support him.

The noises approached nearer still and there was a light. The ghost had a light to see by. Ben could see the ghost's outline. He was wearing a kind of huge cloak. It enveloped his body like a bell. What did he want? What was he going to do with Ben?

The ghost had stopped. He was looking down at Ben. Ben could see his face in the light of the lamp he was carrying. It was a horrible face, dirty and cruel. The ghost was like a man. Ben had not imagined a ghost as a man, but all ghosts had once been people, so it was natural that he should be. 'You, little un. Give me your hand.' It was the ghost who had spoken. Ben pressed his body against the wall. The light stung his eyes. He had to turn away. Ben thought of climbing down. But there was no escape that way. Five steps below him was water.

'Come on. I'm not going to harm you,' the ghost

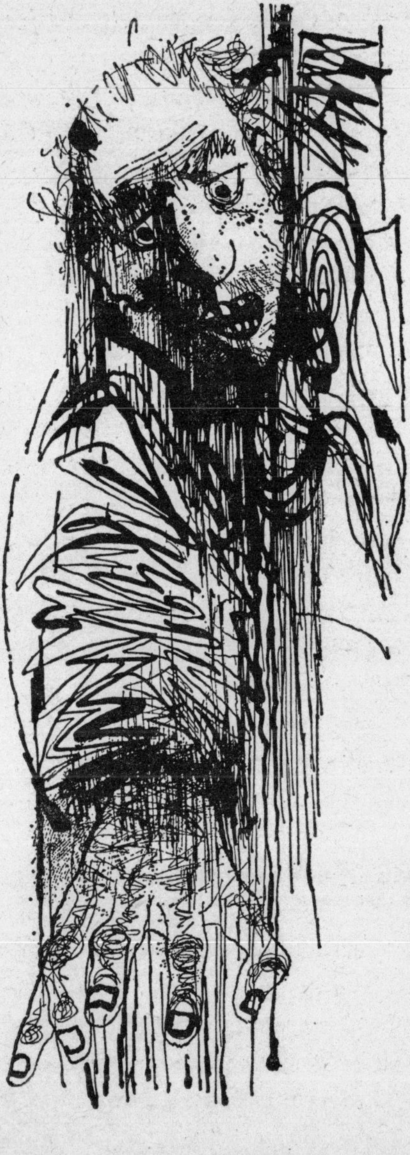

said, reaching out with his hand. Ben tried to shrink away but he could go no further. The ghost's hand came closer.

'Hit him now,' Ben told himself, but his hand holding the brick wouldn't move. It was paralysed. Ben could see the huge hand of the ghost in front of him. There were hairs on it. They were black hairs. The hand touched Ben's pullover. It closed like the claw of a crab and then it pulled. Ben was in a frenzy. 'Get away. Get away from me,' he shrieked.

The ghost recoiled and jumped back. He stood on the ladder doing nothing for a few seconds as though he was thinking, 'What will he do to me now?' Ben wailed to himself. His face was burning hot and his heart was beating like a sledgehammer.

'I've come to take you to your brother,' the ghost said. His voice was quiet. There was almost a note of kindness in it. He talked of Max. What did he mean? How did he know Max? He couldn't have caught Max. Max had gone to the library.

'You give me your arm and I'll help you up,' the ghost said. The hand stretched out again. It felt for Ben's jersey and grasped it. It gripped tightly.

'Don't touch me. Leave me alone,' Ben screamed. He tore with all his might. It didn't make any difference. He could feel himself being dragged. Ben lifted his hand and brought it down as hard as he could. There was a crunching noise as the brick hit the ghost's elbow. The ghost tore his hand away. As he did so he swore loudly. He rubbed the elbow against his chest.

He glared down at Ben, his face screwed up with pain and anger. He'll kill me for that, Ben thought. 'I'll give you one last chance,' the ghost said, 'if you won't come with me, you'll stay here on your own.' He reached out again with his hand. Ben stiffened. He lifted the brick above his head. 'Have it your way then,' the ghost said. He shrugged his shoulders and began climbing upwards. The light became fainter and fainter.

Ben was in darkness once more. He sank back on to the stone. He had won. He had fought the ghost and he had won. But the ghost would return. Ben knew he would. He felt beside him for the other two bricks. They were still there. Perhaps there would be two of them the next time. Well, he would take both of them on. If there was a whole army of ghosts he would fight. And before they took him away there'd be a few broken bones to tell for it.

Ben knew he ought to rest if he was to have any strength left. He felt so weak, and the pain had come in his leg again. He laid his head against the wall and closed his eyes. He did not sleep. That would have been impossible. He was too afraid the ghost might catch him off guard. But of how much time had passed when the noises returned he had no idea.

He sat up, his eyes and ears straining into the blackness. Far above him a dull light had appeared. Ben grasped one of the bricks. The light came closer, illuminating the walls of the shaft. Ben could distinguish the form of a body. But it wasn't on the ladder. It was floating. Ben shivered. And then as if that was not enough he saw another ghost, climbing down the ladder by the floating ghost.

Ben stood up on the stone. He knew he hadn't a chance, not with two of them, but even so he would fight, fight until he could fight no more. The ghosts were nearly upon him now. The one on the ladder wearing the cloak, he was the one who had been there the last time. He was holding the lamp away from his body to show the way for the second ghost. Ben couldn't see the second ghost very well. His face was hidden by his shoes and his arms. Those floating shoes drifted down towards Ben.

Ben drew back his hand and hurled the brick upwards. The ghost on the ladder dodged aside. The brick missed him, hit the wall of the shaft and fell with a splash into the water below. Then there was that same sound of an animal swimming. Ben gave a stifled cry. The floating ghost groped for the ladder just above where the other ghost was standing. Ben reached for another brick. His hands had closed over it when the floating ghost spoke.

'Now stop this nonsense, Ben. It's me. It's Mr Mansion.' They were trying to trick him. That ghost was pretending to be Mr Mansion. They wouldn't catch him so easily. If they wanted to capture him and take him to some strange land, then they were going to have to fight.

'Don't come near me,' Ben screamed. He threw the brick with all his might, but again he missed. There was one brick left. He felt for it clumsily. It was on the edge of the shelf. As he found it he knocked it with his hand and it tumbled from his grasp into the water. Now he had nothing except his bare hands.

'Here, let me get past you,' the ghost who was pretending to be Mr Mansion said. He began to float again.

Ben crouched on the shelf waiting for him. He covered his face with his hands. Strangely enough he was no longer afraid. The second ghost was beside him. Ben could hear his heavy breathing. The ghost was touching him, he was holding his hand.

'It is me, Ben. You have a look for yourself.' The voice was very like Mr Mansion's. Ben opened his fingers wide enough to see through them. The policeman was floating in front of him. He was wearing the dark blue uniform he went to work in.

Ben took his hands from his face. It was Mr Mansion. He wasn't a ghost after all. And he hadn't been floating. There was a rope tied round his waist. It went up the shaft and disappeared into the blackness above where the lamp was. Ben's head reeled. If this was Mr Mansion, then who was the person on the ladder? He couldn't be a ghost either.

Mr Mansion lifted Ben into his arms. The man on the ladder reached out and gave the rope three quick tugs. A moment later they began to ascend in slow, jerky movements. The other man climbed by their side.

Ben could smell the coarse cloth of Mr Mansion's uniform, and he could feel the policeman's whistle through his tunic pocket. It was Mr Mansion. He was safe now. He need do nothing more. He was being carried home to Mum, to Max and to safety. And yet the fear still lingered in his mind, and several times as they rose higher and higher he was seized by a panic that he did not know where he was being taken. But if he was in the hands of ghosts, there wasn't anything he could do about it, so he lay still.

The air in the shaft changed. It became fresher and colder. Ben found himself waking up. He was more aware of what was going on around him. They were at the top of the ladder. Ben saw stars over his head. They sparkled fresh and white in what seemed to Ben a bright blue night sky. Suddenly he felt free. Down below everything had been pressing inwards, the heavy air, the sides of the shaft and the complete stillness and blackness. Now he could see and move as far as he wanted to.

He tried to stand up but the leg he had hurt was too painful. There were people clustering about him. They were all staring at him.

'Is anything the matter with him?' somebody asked.

'He'll be as right as rain in the morning.' It was Mr Mansion speaking. 'All he needs is a hot bath and a good night's rest. I think the rats frightened him more than anything else.' Ben looked up into the faces. Some of them he did not recognize, but Mum was at the front and Max was there as well. Mum was crying. Ben knew she was upset even though he could hardly see her in the dark.

There was a shuffling noise behind them. The man whom Ben thought was a ghost was climbing out of the shaft. A policeman took his hand and helped him to his feet. The man walked over to the crowd of people and stared at Ben. Ben thought for an instant that he saw a strange smile on his face.

For a while they stood round Ben talking to one another in whispers. Then Mum opened a blanket she had on her arm and wrapped it around him. Mr Mansion lifted him into his arms and they all started towards the houses, everybody except the man who had been down the mine with Mr Mansion. Mum stayed behind for a few moments. Ben heard her say, 'Thank you!' Then she hurried after them, leaving the man on his own. He stood watching them as they moved along the slackheaps. Ben turned in Mr Mansion's arms, and when they had almost left the mine behind Ben could still see the man, silhouetted like a tiny insect against the distant sky.

Ben remembered little of the walk home. The cold wind blew in his face. He snuggled close to Mr Mansion's warm tunic, and listened to the crunching feet on the loose coal as he jogged up and down in the policeman's arms. His eyes kept closing even though he wanted to stay awake. He found himself drifting into a sleep, then the cutting wind and Mr Mansion's movements would rouse him again.

'Shall I take him now?' he heard Mum say. Ben looked into Mr Mansion's face and he saw him shake his head.

They crossed the empty building-site and their feet rang out on the hard pavement of the street. Ben tried to sit up to see where he was but Mum laid her hand on his chest and pushed him down again. As they turned into their street Ben could see lights in the windows. People came to their doors and stared out at them as they went past.

'We've found him, Eileen,' Mum called out to one woman. 'I'll tell you about it in the morning.'

Mr and Mrs Johns were standing at the gate when they reached their house. Mrs Johns gave Ben a disapproving glare. 'Causing his mother all that worry!' Ben heard her say. He turned away and saw a black police car standing outside Mr Mansion's house. Then Ben noticed that the other people with them were all policemen. One of them touched Mr Mansion on the arm and said, 'See you tomorrow, Francis.' Ben didn't know Mr Mansion was called Francis. He had not thought of Mr Mansion having a Christian name before that moment. The policeman began to walk towards the car, but then he stopped and gave Ben a pinch on his cheek. 'You're a lucky young fella. Know that, do you?' Ben nodded and smiled.

Mr Mansion carried him up the drive and Mum opened the back door for them. The fire was almost dead in the grate but after the wind outside the room was warm and friendly.

'You run the bath and I'll undress him,' Mr Mansion said. Mum took her coat off and looked into Ben's eyes. There was no expression on her face, and Ben could not tell whether she was angry or not, but he did not think she was.

Mr Mansion laid Ben on the sofa. Max was standing by the mantelpiece, his back to the fire. He hadn't spoken a word since Ben had come out of the mine. Mum told Max to put the kettle on for a cup of tea and then she went through to the bathroom.

As Mr Mansion began to undress him Ben heard the sound of running water. It was like having Dad home again. Ben sat up as Mr Mansion pulled his jersey over his head. There was a thump as something fell on the floor. Mr Mansion picked up the ship and the aeroplane from the floor. The sight of the ship woke Ben a little. But he soon felt sleepy again, and in the bath his head lolled against the hard sides.

He was too tired to stand on his feet and Mr Mansion had to hold him while Mum slipped on his pyjamas. Then Mr Mansion carried him into his bedroom. Max ran on ahead and pulled back the bedcovers. The policeman placed him gently by the wall. 'Would you like a cup of tea, Benny?' Mum said. Her voice seemed to be far away. Ben shook his head. He snuggled into the bed, pulling the sheets and blankets around his body.

Mum placed a finger to her lips and they tiptoed out of the room as quiet as mice. Max was holding the aeroplane in his hand. It reminded Ben of the ship. He looked about the room and just before Mum turned off the light he saw it on the dressing-table, balanced against a pile of comics.

Ben curled himself into a comfortable position. He lay still, his body limp and exhausted. As he drifted into sleep he heard voices from the next room, voices he knew and trusted, and there was the sound of cups as they were placed on saucers.

If you have enjoyed this PICCOLO Book, you may like to choose your next book from the titles listed on the following pages.

Piccolo Fiction

Penelope Lively

ASTERCOTE (illus) 25p

The Cotswold village of Astercote was wiped out in the 14th century by the Black Death – and its ruins now lie hidden in the murky wood. But when Peter and Mair Jenkins discover it, and its secret 'Thing', they find themselves caught up in an atmosphere of medieval superstition that becomes a frightening reality . . .

THE WHISPERING KNIGHTS (illus) 25p

When Martha, William and Susie concoct a magic brew, they unwittingly invoke the enmity of Morgan le Fay, the notorious enchantress who is posing as the wife of a local tycoon. She uses all her powers of evil against them, and only the Whispering Knights and the mysterious Miss Hepplewhite can save them from a terrible fate . . .